Before I die I want to ______________________________.

Before I die I want to ______________________________.

Before I die I want to ______________________________.

Before I die I want to ______________________________.

Before I die I want to ______________________________.

Before I die I want to ______________________________.

Before I die I want to ______________________________.

Before I die I want to ______________________________.

Before I die I want to ______________________________.

Before I die I want to ______________________________.

BEFORE I DIE

BEFORE I DIE

CANDY CHANG

St. Martin's Griffin
New York

DESIGN BY
8½

Before I Die

For information, address St. Martin's Press
175 Fifth Avenue, New York, N.Y. 10010.

Cover and book design by Eight and a Half, NYC
8point5.com

Cover Photo by Francis Allen
Illustrations by Jeff Scher
Map by Melanie Burke

candychang.com
beforeidie.cc
www.stmartins.com

First published in the United States
by St. Martin's Griffin
First St. Martin's Griffin Edition:
November 2013

Library of Congress Cataloging-in-Publication
data available upon request

ISBN 978-1-250-02084-0

10 9 8 7 6 5 4 3 2 1

for Joan & James

We make our world significant by the courage of our questions and the depth of our answers.

— CARL SAGAN

Introduction

Randal Ford

Joan died on a quiet August day. She was a mother to me for fifteen years. She was kind and thoughtful. She loved to garden and she taught me how to plant flowers. When I was a confused teenager, she told me to be true to myself. Her death was sudden and unexpected, and there were so many things she still wanted to do: learn to play the piano, live in Paris, and see the Pacific Ocean. I spent a long time filled with grief. Then I felt gratitude for the time we had together.

Death was always on my mind. It brought clarity to my life. It reminded me of the people I want to love well, the type of person I want to become, and the things I want to do. But I struggled to maintain this perspective. It's easy to get caught up in the day-to-day and forget what really matters to me. I wondered if other people felt the same way.

Over the years I've asked questions in public space to share more with my neighbors. This one was personal as my own priorities changed. With help from old and new friends, I painted an abandoned house in my neighborhood with chalkboard paint and stenciled it with a grid of the sentence, "Before I die I want to ________." Anyone walking by could pick up a piece of chalk, reflect on their lives, and share their personal aspirations in public. It was an experiment and I didn't know what to expect. By the next day, the wall was bursting with handwritten responses and it kept growing.

Before I die I want to sing for millions, plant a tree, hold her one more time, eat a salad with an alien, build a school, straddle the International Date Line, live off the grid, abandon all insecurities, be completely myself...

People's hopes and dreams made me laugh out loud and they made me tear up.

People's hopes and dreams made me laugh out loud and they made me tear up. They consoled me during my toughest times. I understood my neighbors in new and enlightening ways, and I discovered the strength of the wall: it reminded me that I'm not alone as I try to make sense of my life.

If you're holding this book, you know the Before I Die wall became popular, far more popular than I could have ever imagined. Seemingly overnight, my inbox exploded with earnest messages from students, widowers, artists, business owners, activists, community leaders, coworkers, neighbors, and friends around the world who wanted to make a wall with their community. My friends and I created a toolkit and website to help people along the way, and now over two hundred Before I Die walls have been created in over ten languages and in over thirty countries, including Kazakhstan, Argentina, China, Italy, and South Africa.

In the following pages, you'll see walls that appeared on construction sites, campuses, vacant lots, plazas, buildings, and the spaces between. This happened thanks to incredibly passionate people who invested their time, money, and sweat to provide a place for their community to share more with one another. Their walls and stories have been a constant source of inspiration and therapy for me, and you'll read more from them about their experience. Each wall is unique and reflects the people of that neighborhood. Each wall is a tribute to living an examined life. And by using a few simple tools like chalkboard paint, stencils, and spray paint, it shows you don't need a big budget to make a big impact.

These public yet anonymous walls are an honest mess of the longing, pain, joy, insecurity, gratitude, fear, and wonder you find in any neighborhood. You'll see the handwritten responses of citizens far and wide and read some of their stories. You'll also see some of my favorite responses on these unbridled walls, from driving an ice cream truck to overcoming depression. In the end, the power of this project rests in the hands of the passerby who picks up a piece of chalk, pauses for a moment, and writes something honest, poetic, and occasionally heartbreaking.

Death is something we're often discouraged to talk about or even think about: *Don't go there. It's too sad. You don't need to think about it until you're older.* Perhaps this is why it took me so long to explore these thoughts, but when I finally did, I found a comfort and clarity that I did not expect. Beyond the tragic truth of mortality lies a bright calm that reminds me of my place in the world. When I think about death, the mundane things that stress me out are reduced to their small and rightful place; the things that matter most to me become big and crisp again. Regularly contemplating death, as Stoics and other philosophers encourage, is a powerful tool to restore perspective and remember the things that make your life meaningful. Thinking about death clarifies your life.

In our age of digital distraction, it's more important than ever to find ways to maintain perspective and remember that life is brief and tender. It's easy to go with the flow and postpone our deepest needs. It's easy to take the people we love for granted and leave things unsaid. And it's far too easy to neglect our relationship with ourselves. The mythologist Joseph Campbell once said, "The privilege of a lifetime is being who you are." To be true to ourselves, we need to take the time to step back, pause, be quiet, and reflect as we continue to grow and change. With every experience, we gain new perspectives that can reshape our guiding star.

Our public spaces are as profound as we allow them to be. They are our shared spaces and reflect what matters to us as a community and as individuals. The historian Lewis Mumford once wrote that the origins of society were not just for physical survival but for sacred things that offer "a more valuable and meaningful kind of life." At their greatest, our public spaces can nourish our well-being and help us see that we're not alone as we try to make sense of our lives. They can help us grieve together and celebrate together and console one another and be alone together. Each passerby is another person full of longing, anxiety, fear, and wonder. With more ways to share in public space, the people around us can not only help us make better places, they can help us become our best selves.

Candy

The House

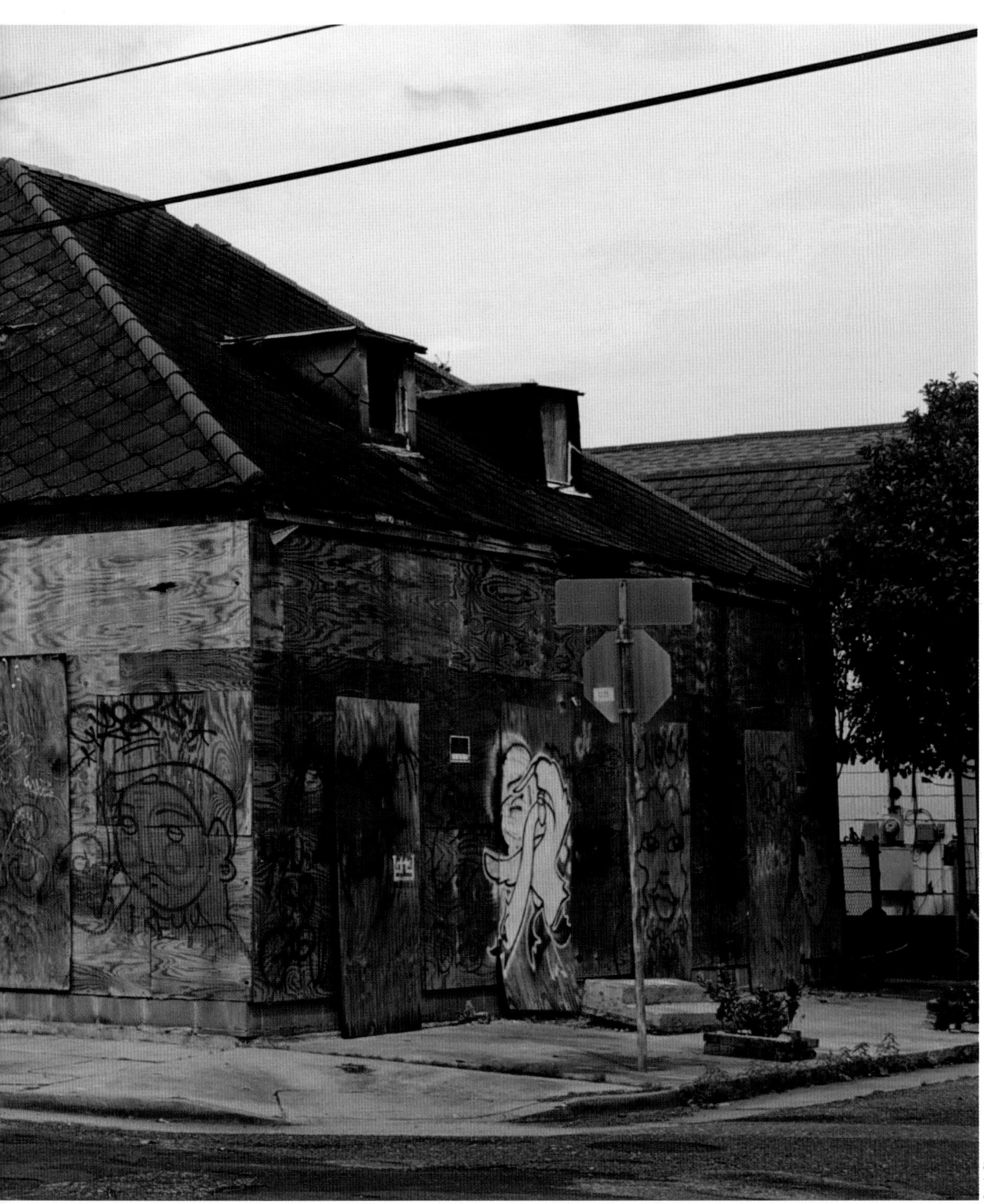

Candy Chang

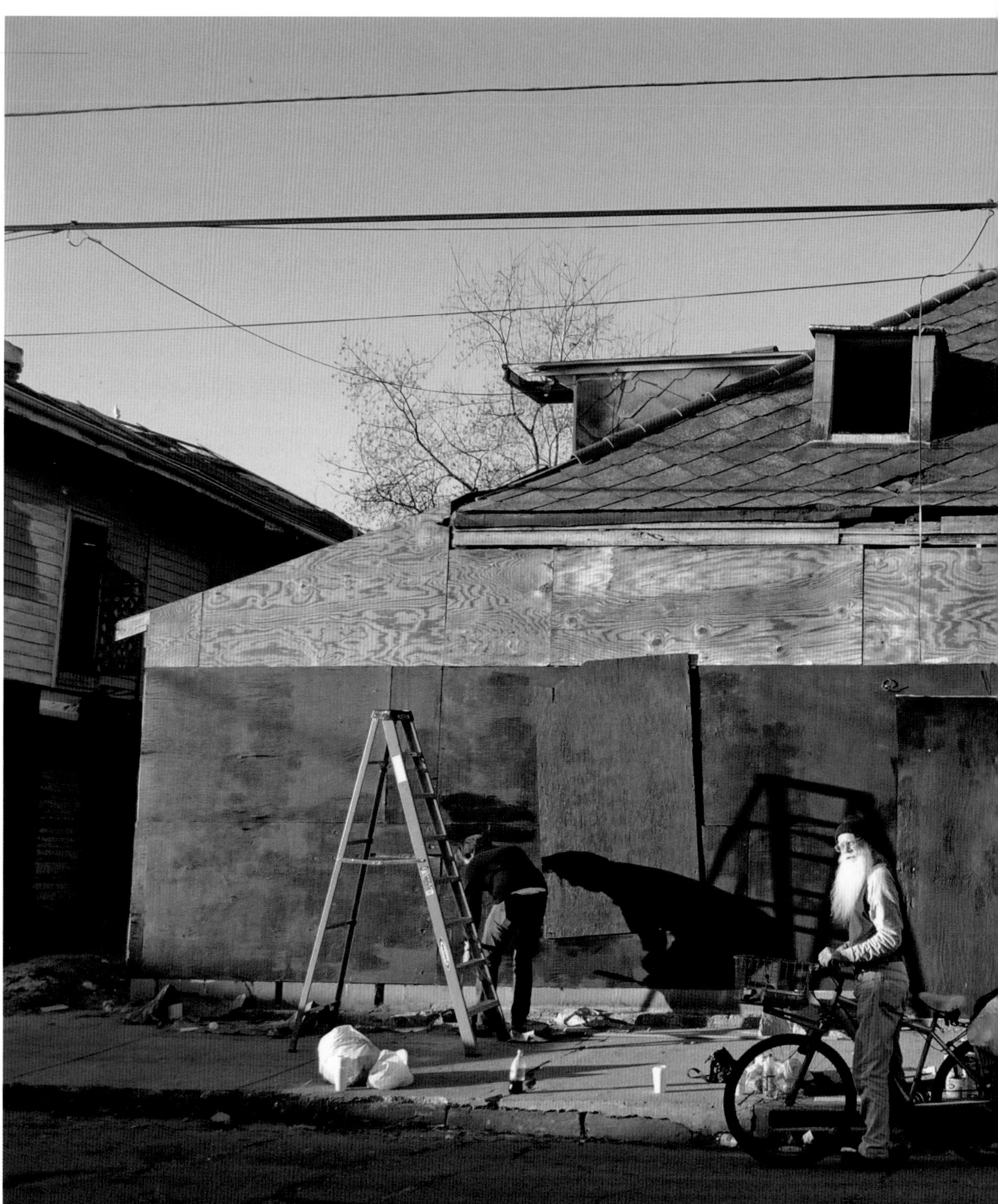

Candy Chang

Before I die...
LOVE
OWN A BOAT
SEE EQUALITY
Be published

REGRET NOTHING.
MEET MR. WHISKERS!
COMMUNIZE.
Kiss my wife
LEARN TO BREATHE
STOP HIDING

Candy Chang

GETTYS
ROOFING & CONSTRUCTION
504-277-6627 · 985-847-2002
504-377-4200
GETTYS

Candy Chang

Candy Chang

MY HOMEMADE STENCIL

James A. Reeves

POKER WAS INVENTED HERE
HAS MORE HISTORIC DISTRICTS ON THE NATIONAL REGISTER THAN ANY OTHER U.S. CITY
POPULATION: 360,740

New Orleans
Louisiana

organized by
CANDY CHANG

I live in New Orleans and I am in love with New Orleans. My soul is always soothed by the giant live oak trees that have shaded lovers, drunks, and dreamers for hundreds of years. And I trust a city that makes way for music. It seems like every time someone sneezes, New Orleans has a parade. This city has some of the most beautiful architecture in the world, yet it also has one of the highest amounts of abandoned properties in America. I lived two blocks from a house that had been collecting dust and graffiti for years.

Making the first Before I Die wall was a three-month odyssey that might not have happened if that house wasn't in such bad shape. Before beginning this experiment, I wanted to respect the people who lived nearby. It's not common to propose a project that invites people to write in public space. I promised I would maintain the wall every day and if it didn't work out, I would paint over the whole thing. My neighborhood's blight committee supported anything that might prevent the historic house from being demolished. The homeowner, a single mother whose big dreams fell through due to crooked contractors, said, please go ahead. Neighbors on the block said, "It can't be worse than it is right now," and offered to help.

James A. Reeves

I printed the phrase "Before I die I want to ______" on a few sheets of paper, glued them to a piece of poster board, and cut out the letters with a blade. I woke up early one morning in January and with help from old and new friends, I painted the weatherboards of this crumbling house with primer and chalkboard paint. An elderly man with a wizard's beard stopped and reminisced about the history of the block. People walking their children and dogs thanked us for doing something with that eyesore. The head of the blight committee brought us a plate of tea and cookies. A neighbor across the street said it looked a hundred times better already.

Then a police car stopped. The officer told us a resident filed a complaint and we needed a permit. I called city departments and a colorful man told me I didn't need a permit. "That's the way the banana bends," he said, "and if anyone doesn't like it, you can tell them to cram it." A local organization told me a permit was required because it was considered a mural. I presented my proposal to three civic committees at City Hall. They responded with open minds and granted me an official "Certificate of Appropriateness" to post on the wall.

One month after painting the wall, we returned to finish it. Drivers honked their horns and said right on. A man dressed like a pirate told us jokes and wrote, "Before I die I want to be tried for piracy." We nailed some containers onto the wall and filled them with chalk. The block doesn't have heavy foot traffic so I didn't know how many people would notice the wall. Would passersby understand they were invited to write on the side of the house? Maybe it would be covered in graffiti overnight. I didn't know what to expect. But I was pleased with how it looked and because it was cheap to make, it was no big deal if it didn't work out.

Candy Chang

THE HEAD OF MY NEIGHBORHOOD BLIGHT COMMITTEE BRINGS US A PLATE OF TEA AND COOKIES

The next day I was blown away. All eighty lines were filled and responses spilled into the margins. The replies were thoughtful, funny, poetic, and heartbreaking: Before I die I want to see my students become teachers, write a book, love recklessly again, understand, be ok with not understanding, be a YouTube sensation, cook a soufflé, know who I am, see all homeless people with homes, go to the Galapagos Islands, feel like the only girl in the room. These were the first responses on the wall and I am forever grateful to these people who were so open and sincere, setting the tone for the thousands of responses that followed.

During the next seven months, we documented the wall, washed it, and replenished it with chalk. People young and old picked up a piece of chalk. People shared quietly and loudly. People cried alone and laughed together. Neighbors introduced themselves to one another in front of the wall while reading through the day's responses. Cars and buses pulled over and people posed to take photos in front of the wall. This neglected space had become a constructive one, and people who ordinarily had little to do with one another began taking care of it. "People are around all the time," said the grandmother who lived across the street. "The block is safer now."

Concerns about a public chalkboard were answered as the project unfolded. No one ever wrote beyond the wall. There were a handful of wise-ass comments, but people erased them and they were eclipsed by the thousands of sincere responses that made people laugh, cry, and think a little more deeply about their lives. I learned so much about the people around me and how much I wasn't alone as I struggled — and still struggle — to make sense of my own life.

I also learned there will always be an angry neighbor. Amidst the hopes to build schools and long-

THE FIRST STENCIL ON THE WALL

Kristina Kassem

ings to see sons and daughters come back from the war, someone pulled out the chalk holders every few days and crushed them in a patch of yard next to the house. Anonymous neighbors kindly donated their own boxes and buckets of chalk and wrote vows to find the mystery "chalk thief" on the wall. The chalk thief didn't stop us. He helped us design tougher chalk holders.

Abandoned buildings have become such a common sight that they often slip quietly into the backdrop of our cities like an accepted part of our landscape. But people paid closer attention to that shuttered old house as it absorbed our hopes and dreams for seven months. People asked questions: How old is it? Who owned it? What will happen to it? The house was trying very hard to stay up until someone cared for it again. That time finally came when a new owner bought the property. We painted over the wall to make way for the construction crew. I stenciled one last sentence, something actor and New Orleans native Wendell Pierce said a few months earlier: "Our thoughts are to the individual as our art is to the community." And then the first Before I Die wall ended for the happiest of reasons. Today, the house has become a home again.

made with love by CANDY CHANG, KRISTINA KASSEM, CORY KLEMMER, ANAMARIA VIZCAINO, ALAN WILLIAMS, JAMES REEVES, ALEX VIALOU, EARL CARLSON, RON MORRISON, AND GARY HUSTWIT. WITH PERMISSION AND SUPPORT FROM THE PROPERTY OWNER, RESIDENTS OF THE BLOCK, THE NEIGHBORHOOD ASSOCIATION'S BLIGHT COMMITTEE, THE HISTORIC DISTRICT LANDMARKS COMMISSION, THE ARTS COUNCIL, AND THE CITY PLANNING COMMISSION

James A. Reeves

Before I die I want to...

be tried for piracy.

Before I die I want to...

be someone's cavalry.

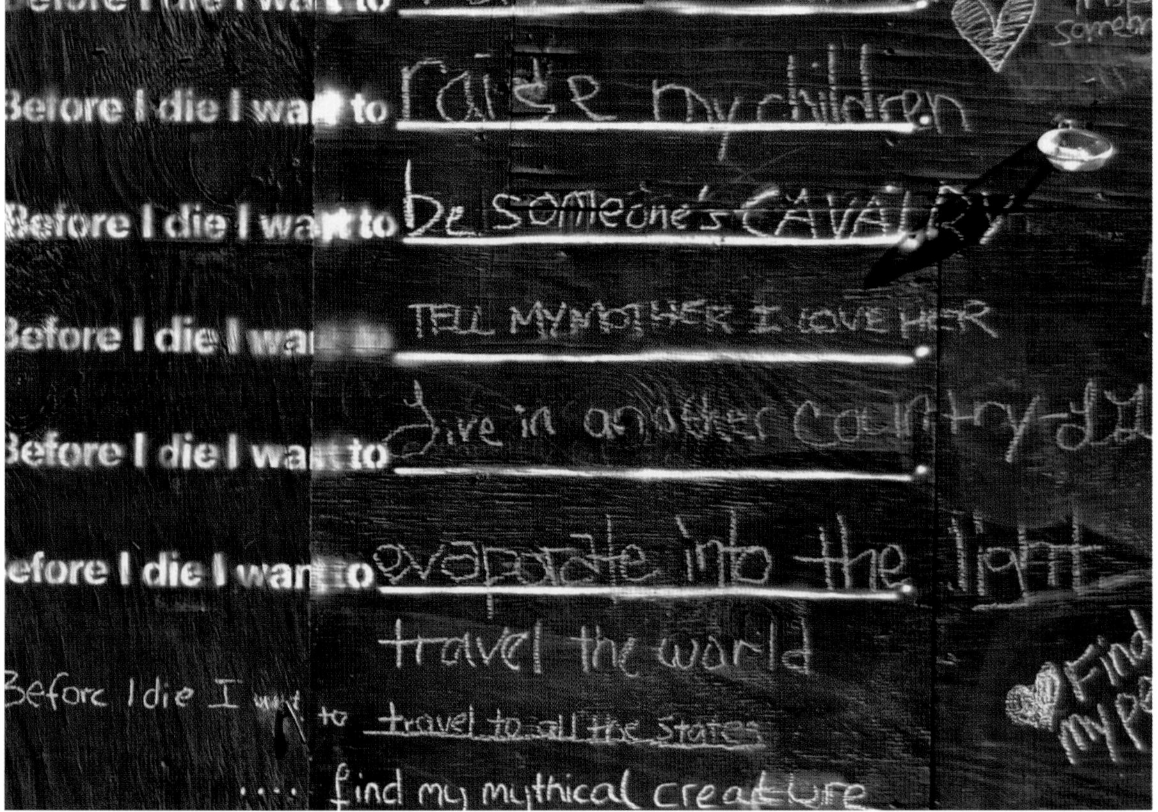

Before I die I want to raise my children
Before I die I want to be someone's CAVALRY
TELL MY MOTHER I LOVE HER
Before I die I want to live in another country
evaporate into the light
travel the world
Before I die I want to travel to all the states
find my mythical creature

Kristina Kassem

Before I die I want to...

love recklessly again.

Before I die I want to Go to the Galapagos Islands
Before I die I want to BEAT SENSE IN TO YOU
Before I die I want to UNDERSTAND
Before I die I want to Be ok with NOT understanding
Before I die I want to write a book
Before I die I want to HIKE THE APPALACHIAN TRAIL
Before I die I want to live for ever
fall in love
world Peace
2nd best
SMOKE CRACK
LIVE

James A. Reeves

Before I die I want to...

eat a salad with an alien.

Before I die I want to...

sing for millions.

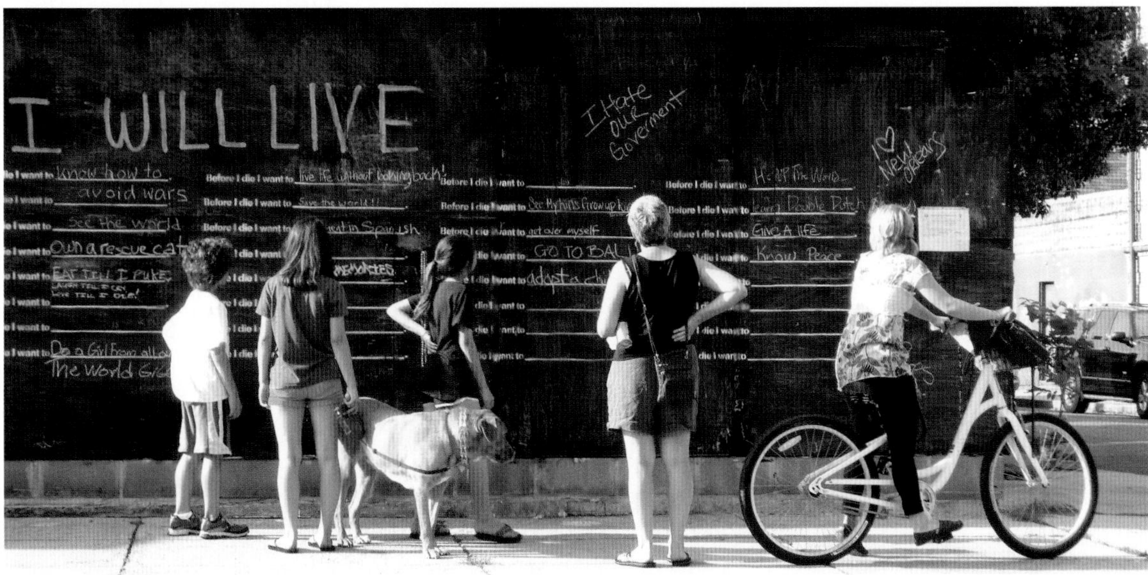

Before I die I want to...

straddle the International Date Line.

Before I die I want to...

see my daughter graduate.

Before I die I want to...

teach my grandkids to garden.

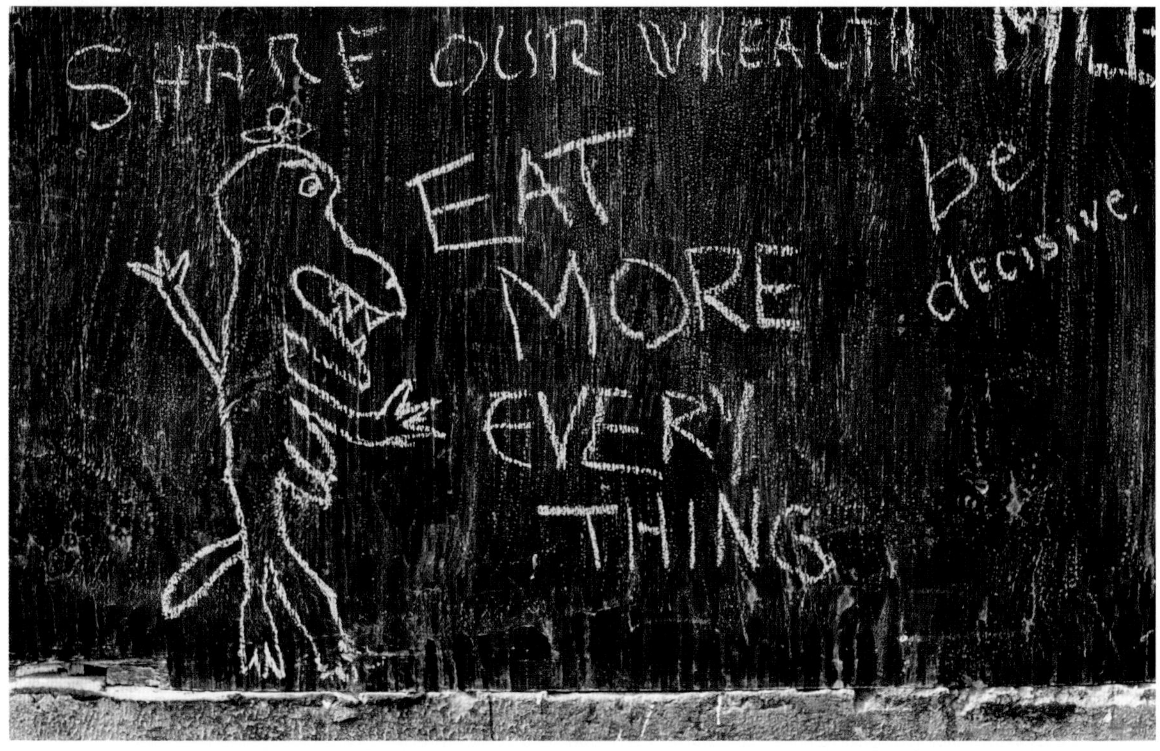

Before I die I want to...

have a student come back and tell me it mattered.

to live for ever
LIKE A
MAKE IT TO DINNER TODAY
to Be Completely myself.

Before I die I want to...

see the leaves change many times.

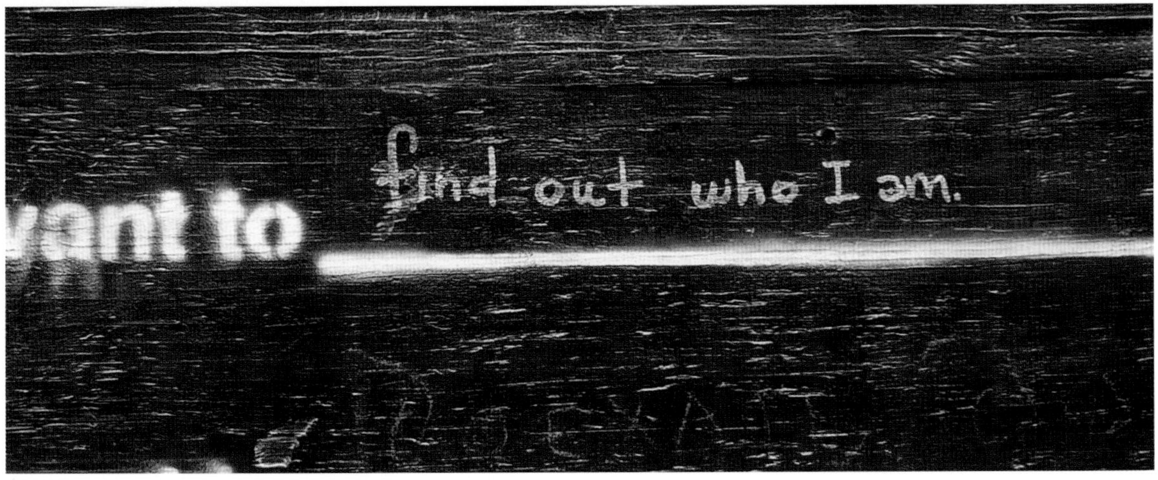

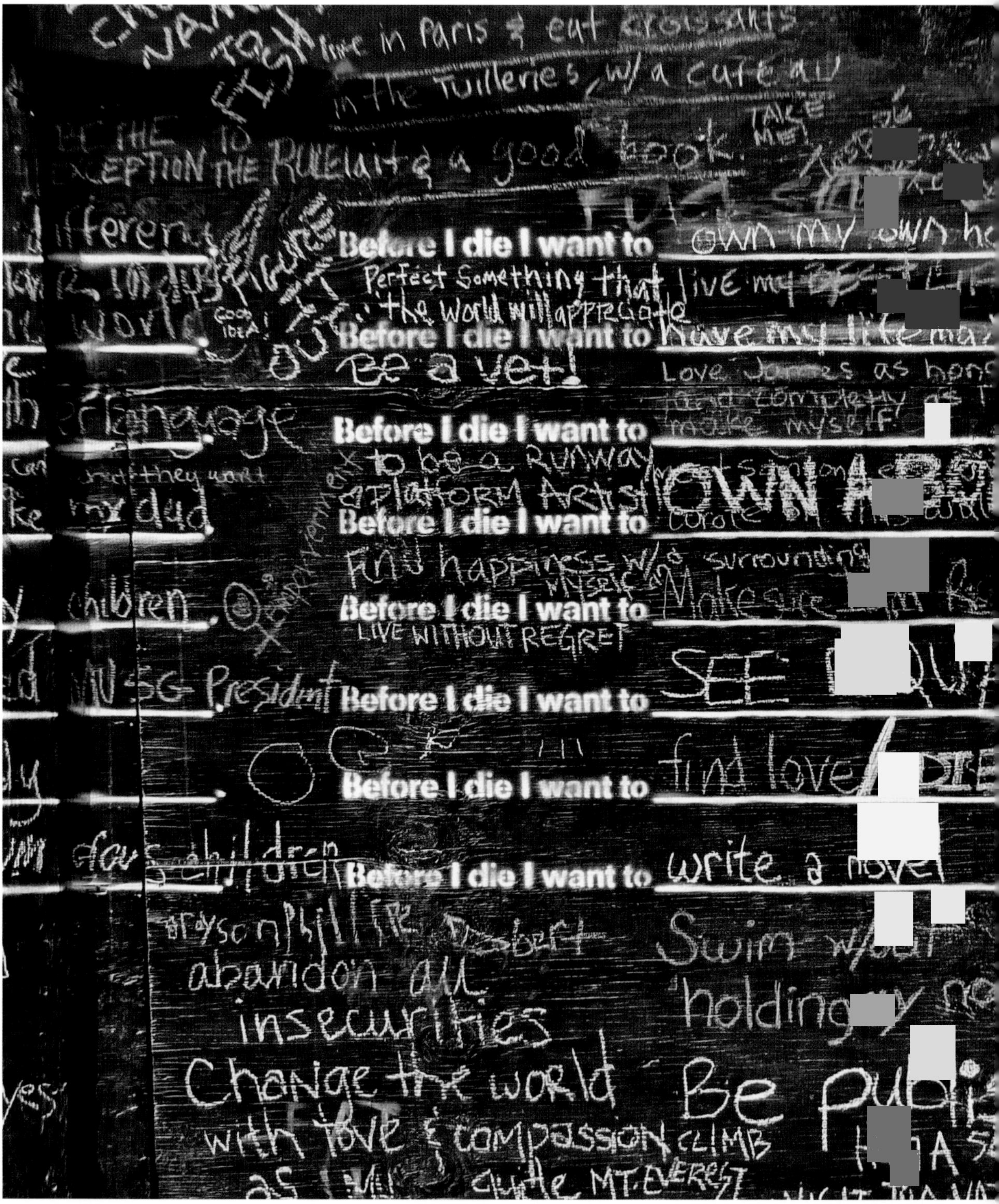
live in Paris & eat croissants
in the Tuilleries w/ a cute guy
Be the exception to the rule
write a good book
Before I die I want to
Perfect Something that the world will appreciate
Before I die I want to
Be a vet!
Before I die I want to
to be a Runway Platform Artist
Before I die I want to
Find happiness w/o myself
Before I die I want to
LIVE WITHOUT REGRET
MUSG President
Before I die I want to
SEE
Before I die I want to
find love
Before I die I want to
write a novel
abandon all insecurities
Change the world with love & compassion
CLIMB MT. EVEREST

See The change
Hug a panda bear
Before I die I want to
not be afraid of
Before I die I want to Name a Star
Before I die I want to
Bring my kids to NOLA
how to read
Before I die I want to
become a human rights activist in a developing country
Before I die I want to love and be loved
be decisive
Before I die I want to live w/ the Amish
See New Orleans thrive
Before I die I want to plant a tree
Before I die I want to Make the world a better place
Swim in a pool of Golden Retriever puppies!
To be the one that She believes
live ABROAD
Give

Candy Chang

Candy Chang

Before I die I want to...

read the full Constitution.

Before I die I want to...

eat all the candy and sushi in the world.

Kristina Kassem

Before I die I want to...

hold her one more time.

Before I die I want to...

write a bedtime story.

Before I die I want to...

abandon all insecurities

Before I die ...
LIVE WITHOUT REGRET!
(PEACE)
BUILD A FOOTPATH TO ALGIERS
ATLANTIS!
to LIVE!
Believe
Before I die I want to feel at home
Before I die I want to be a mother
Before I die I want to live in an old house
Before I die I want to Witness A Miracle
Before I die I want to adopt a child
Before I die I want to be me
Before I die I want to
Before I die I want to Live
TO SEE ITALY
DANCE!
BE RICH!
Be Famous!
WIN
FORGIVE MY PARENTS FOR THEIR SHORTCOMINGS
BECOME A MERMAID

Candy Chang

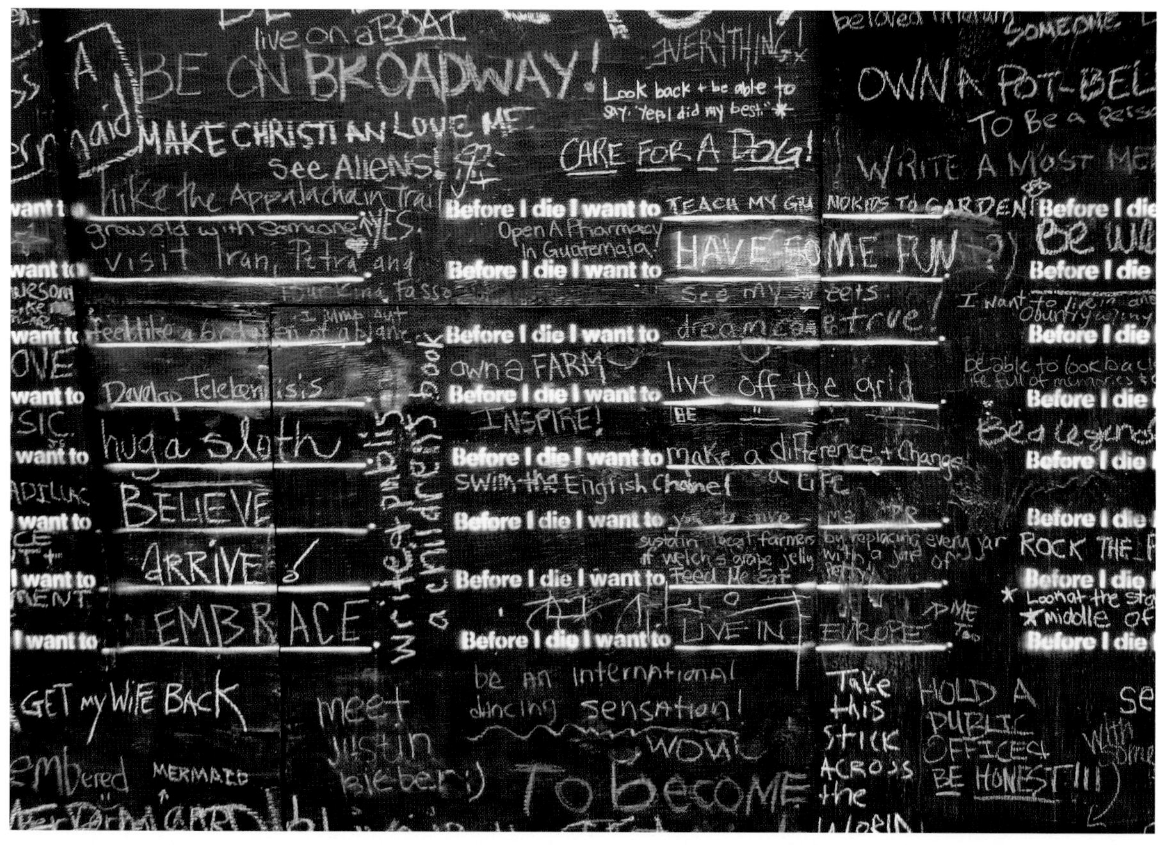

Before I die I want to...

help my neighbor.

SEE WHAT I'M LIKE
AS AN OLD MAN.
EVERYTHING I'VE DONE SO FAR
BIGGER, BETTER, FASTER
have many adventures
see my daughter
marry & live happily ever after
and spoil my grand kids.

Candy Chang

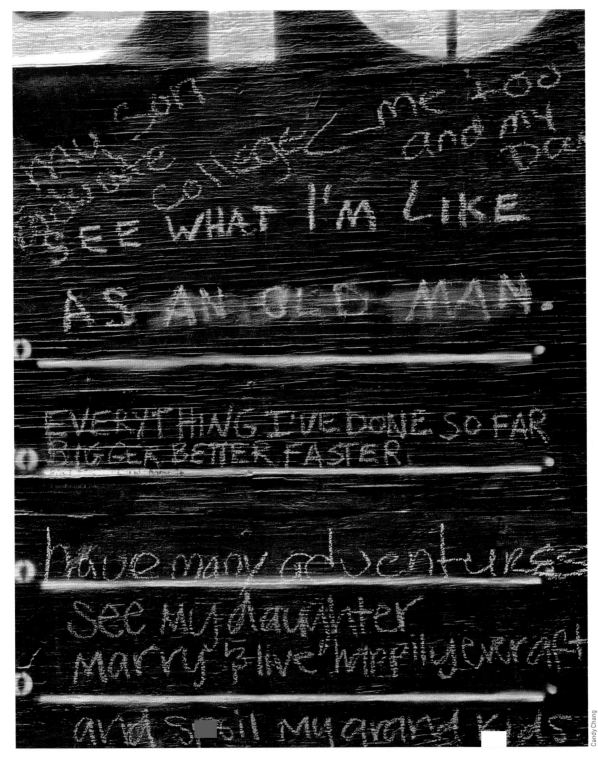

Before I die I want to...

truly make a difference in someone's life.

ERIC'S STORY

My story is like others in the area. I lost my house and much of my community in Hurricane Katrina, and a month prior I lost my brother to suicide. I became numb. I happened to discover the Before I Die wall by accident one day and it changed my life. Seeing so many emotions left by complete strangers on such an "un-beautiful" house in New Orleans reassured me that beauty is everywhere. Now I continue to move on, looking for beauty in the world and helping others see that there is a reason to live despite the obstacles that life throws at us. My passion is showing everyone who is struggling that there is hope in tomorrow.

Candy Chang

Eric Nunez

Before I die I want to...

see
New Orleans
thrive.

WALLS AROUND THE WORLD

Featured walls at a glance.

Valdez, Alaska p.230
Minneapolis, Minnesota p.152
Montreal, Canada p.158
Lexington, Massachusetts p.132
Dublin, Ireland p.110
Chicago, Illinois p.92
Milwaukee, Wisconsin p.148
Portsmouth, New Hampshire p.174
Vancouver, Canada p.232
Brooklyn, New York p.76
Black Rock City, Nevada p.72
Jersey City, New Jersey p.120
Reno, Nevada p.190
New Orleans, Louisianna p.16
Washington, D.C. p.238
San Francisco, California p.198
Newport News, Virginia p.164
Charleston, South Carolina p.86
Querétaro, Mexico p.182
Savannah, Georgia p.212
Xalapa, Mexico p.244
Madrid, Spain p.142
Trujillo, Peru p.228
Lisbon, Portugal p.136
Sao Paulo, Brazil p.210
Córdoba, Argentina p.100
Asunción, Paraguay p.58
Santiago, Chile p.206
N
W
E
S

THERE ARE 48 WALLS FEATURED IN THE CHAPTER. AT THE TIME OF THIS BOOK'S PUBLICATION, THERE ARE OVER 200 WALLS ALL OVER THE WORLD.

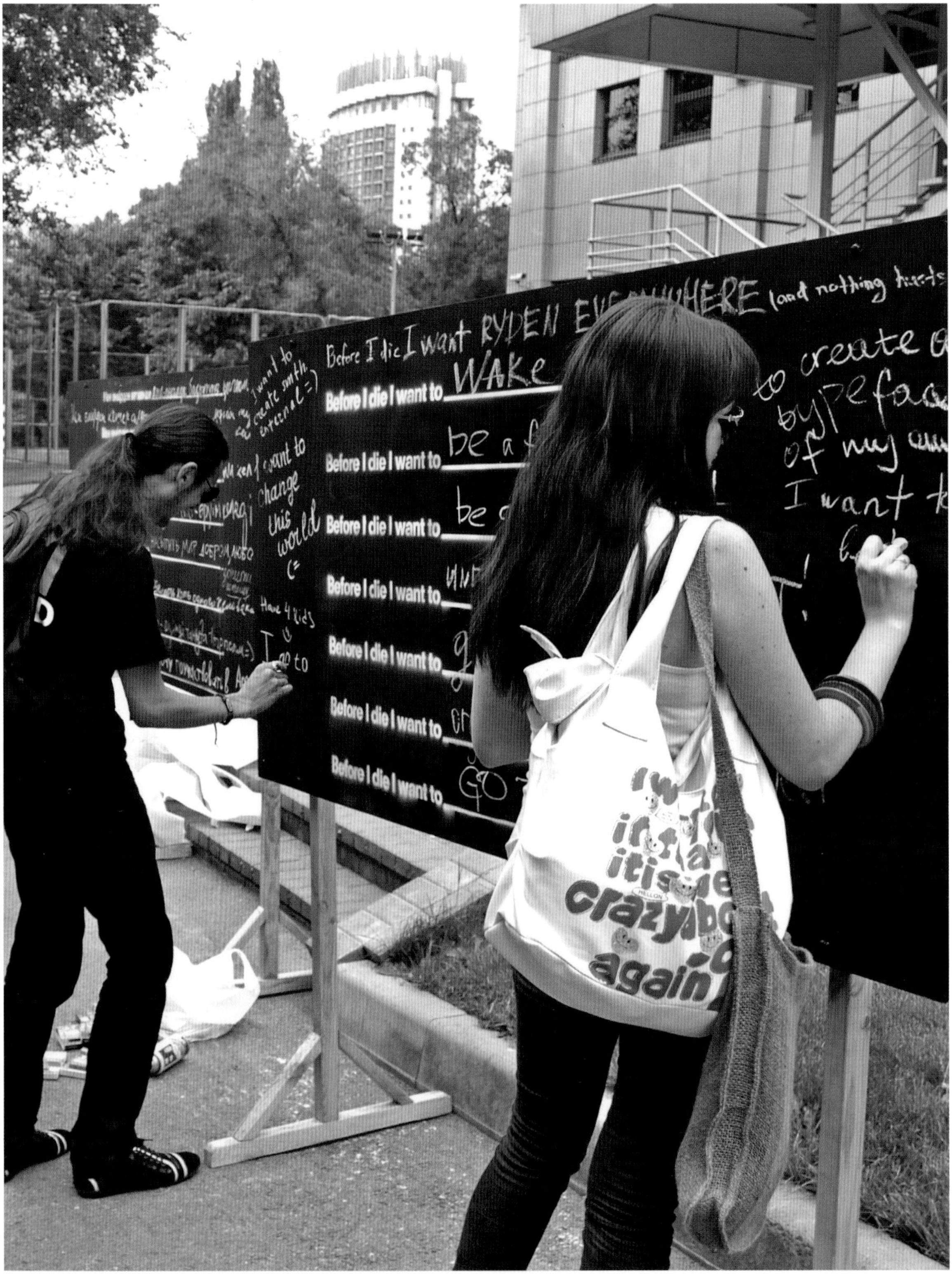

Candy Chang

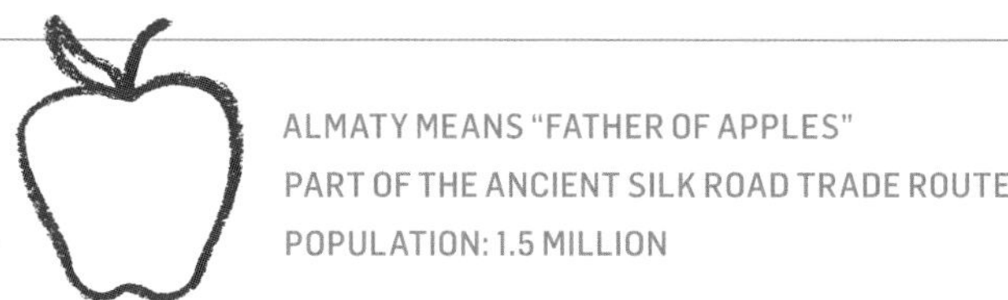

ALMATY MEANS "FATHER OF APPLES"
PART OF THE ANCIENT SILK ROAD TRADE ROUTE
POPULATION: 1.5 MILLION

Almaty

Kazakhstan

organized by
YOUTH ART CAMP

On a soft spring day I arrived in Kazakhstan, where big green mountains and bigger white mountains hug the city of Almaty. This became the beautiful backdrop of the second Before I Die installation. The conference team built three freestanding chalkboards, and together we stenciled them in Kazakh, Russian, and English. After I gave a talk, everyone gathered around the boards, where people read, laughed, and wrote, while others gave their friends piggyback rides. The board collected hopes to "create a typeface of my own," "travel around the world by foot," "make my parents proud," and "understand myself." Aidar Marat, an architect who helped build the chalkboards, was surprised by how sincere some of the people were when responding. "Maybe because it's anonymous, that's the beauty. Shy people can express their feelings too. It's kind of like therapy. They can release some stuff that they were holding in."

made with love by LUDMILA TSOY, ALEXANDRA TSAY, AIDAR MARAT, RUSLAN LYAN, YEKATERINA SYRTSOVA, SHOLPAN SULEIMENOVA, MIKHAIL KOVAL, AND XENIYA MEDVEDEVA

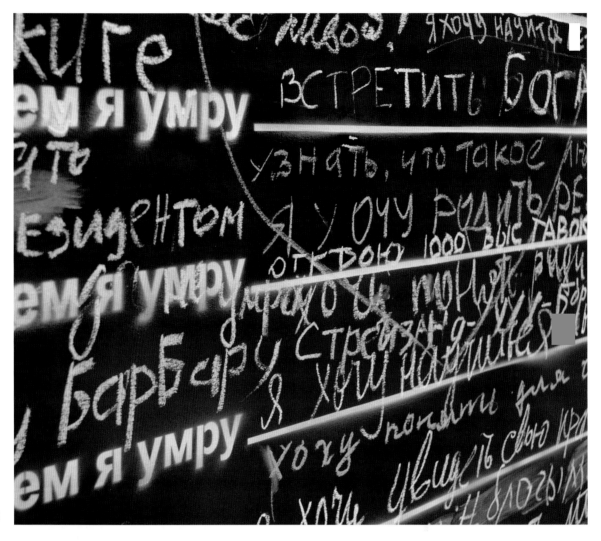

Before I die I want to...

organize 1000 exhibitions.

Before I die I want to...

visit Amsterdam and New Orleans.

Before I die I want to...

create a typeface of my own.

Before I die I want to...

learn to be brave.

Before I die I want to...

be the last romantic on the planet.

Candy Chang

Jaime Torales

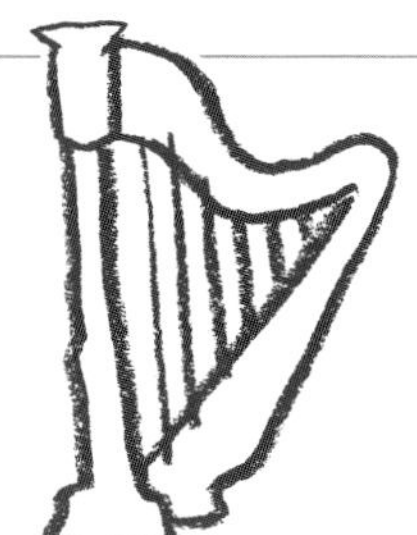

HOSTS THE WORLD HARP FESTIVAL
SITE OF THE FIRST RAILROAD IN SOUTH AMERICA
POPULATION: 1.9 MILLION

Asunción
Paraguay

organized by
UNIVERSIDAD NACIONAL DE ASUNCIÓN

How nice to be able to say you live in the Mother of Cities. That's the nickname for Asunción, the largest city in Paraguay and one of the oldest cities in South America. As part of a school project, students at Universidad Nacional de Asunción created two walls in Spanish and Guaraní to serve their bilingual community. They set up one in an abandoned old port where people go to walk by the river, and the other in a new park still under construction. "I watched a bunch of people write, and it felt great knowing I was helping others express themselves," said organizer Osvaldo Cristaldo. "As for me, I didn't write anything on the wall. At first it was because I wanted to leave room for others, but then I realized it was because I was trying to figure out what to write. It's something I've been thinking about since we started building it, and honestly, that's the experiment's impact on me. That I'm still thinking about it."

made with love by OSVALDO CRISTALDO, LUJAN ROJAS POLETTI, MARIA GLAUSER, PUERTO ABIERTO, PATY IBARROLA, JAIME TORALES, TATSUMI SOSA, ARTURO VALIENTE, DIEGO RECALDE, GIANINNA MORINIGO, HORACIO FRANCO, FLIA. ROJAS POLETTI, TORNERIA SAN FRANCISCO

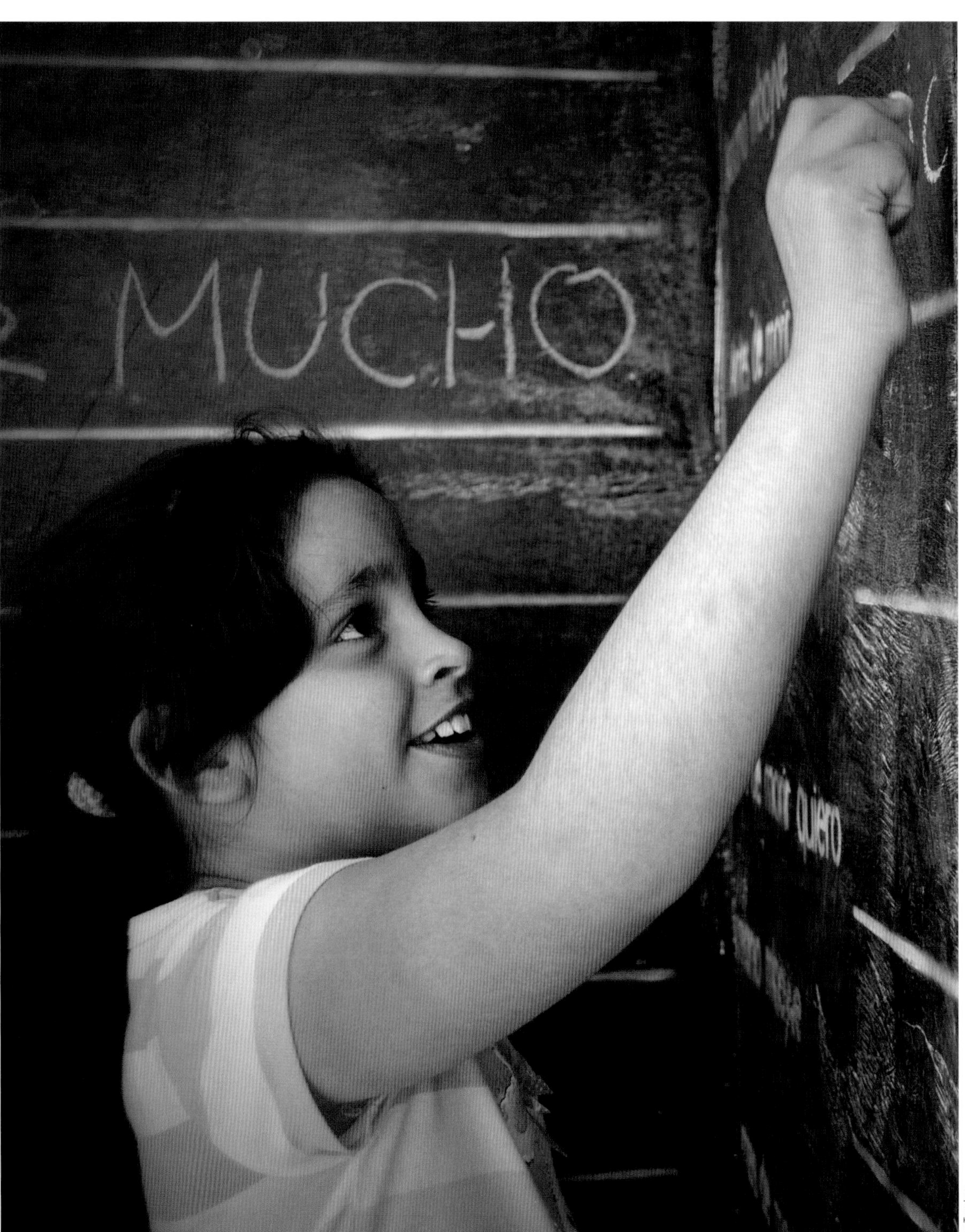

Jaime Torales

Before I die I want to...

learn as much as I can.

Before I die I want to...

see a Paraguay without corruption.

Before I die I want to...

have seven children.

Before I die I want to...

own an ice cream factory.

Before I die I want to...

not be forgotten.

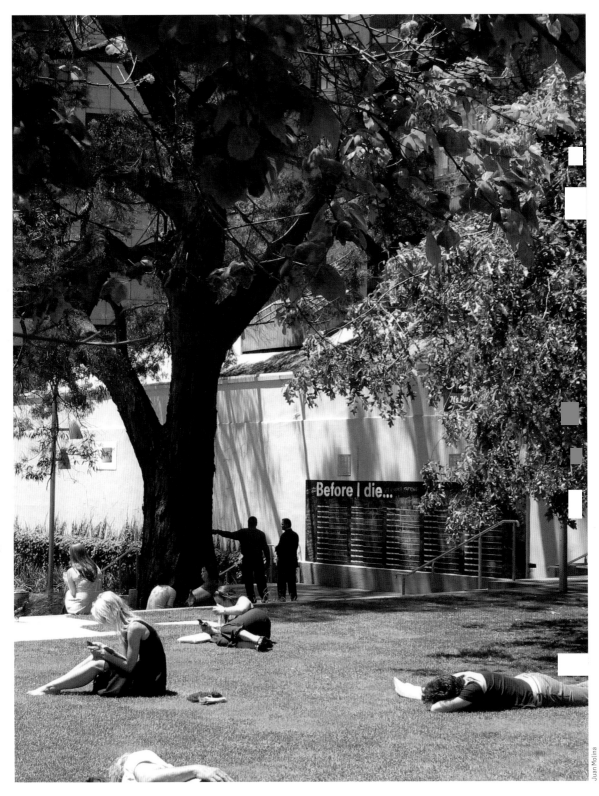

Juan Molina

KNOWN AS THE CITY OF SAILS
HOME TO 50 VOLCANOS
POPULATION: 1.3 MILLION

Auckland
New Zealand

organized by
JUAN MOLINA & SOPHIE ISLER

Six days after the death of his father, architect Juan Molina learned about the Before I Die project and decided to make a wall. "I came to realize that before I die I want to be ready. You're the only one who knows what it will take to help you achieve this." With the blessing of the property owner, civic groups, and St. Patrick's Cathedral, he installed a wall in St Patrick's Square in the city center. "It suited the wall perfectly since it's one of the first urban public spaces in contemporary Auckland. I loved the light in the afternoon through the trees. The wall always filled up fast and the corridor came to life." For one month, the wall collected hopes from "be a singing sensation" to "see my grandpa." When Juan told me why he made the wall, I was deeply touched. "After my father died, I was not able to go home to Spain immediately," he said. "During that time, the wall somehow became an important part of my grieving journey."

made with love by JUAN MOLINA, SOPHIE ISLER, ANTONIO CALIARI-PEARCE, GABRIELLE MUNRO, MIKE LOWE, NADINE ISLER, ADAM WINDSHIP, DANIEL PORUS, GARY BUYN, SEING CHOOI, BLAIR CRESSY, WITH THANKS TO REDDY GROUP, THE ST. PATRICKS CATHEDRAL, RESENE PAINTS, AND CPRW FISHER ARCHITECTS

Before I die I want to...

see, hear, know, and feel peace.

Juan Molina

Before I die I want to...

discover the cure for cancer.

Before I die I want to...

become a pilot.

Before I die I want to...

take less and give more.

Before I die I want to...

visit Venice with the love of my life.

Before I die I want to...

live like a king.

Chad Buckwalter

CALLED THE BICYCLE CAPITAL OF THE WORLD
TIANANMEN SQUARE IS THE WORLD'S LARGEST PUBLIC SQUARE
POPULATION: 17.8 MILLION

Beijing
China

organized by
CHAD BUCKWALTER, THE BJ REVIEWER & BEIJING FORESTRY UNIVERSITY

"In China, school days are twelve to fourteen hours long," explained Chad Buckwalter, who teaches middle school and high school students at an English learning center. "After regular school, kids go to English learning centers for more lessons." The class heard about the project and wanted to put up a board, so they got approval to make a wall at the university. They were worried people wouldn't write on it, but that didn't become a problem. "I couldn't clean it fast enough," said Chad. "Students here have a lot to say and not a lot of places to say it, so it's neat to give them this opportunity. One time we took away the chalk because of bad weather. Somehow someone found a piece and wrote in Chinese, 'Freedom of speech is a form of democracy. Take the time each day to do it.'"

made with love by CHAD BUCKWALTER, THEBJREVIEWER.COM, BEIJING FORESTRY UNIVERSITY EASY AND NEW LANGUAGE TRAINING CENTER, JUN WANG, ESTHER WU, LUCY, JAMES, HANNAH, JIM, JENNIFER, HANNAH, TINA, ARTHUR, TONY, CARL, EASON, PETER

Sarah Clement

HOSTS AN ANNUAL FAIRY TALE FESTIVAL
THE BERLIN WALL ONCE SEPARATED WEST BERLIN FROM THE REST OF GERMANY
POPULATION: 3.5 MILLION

Berlin
Germany

organized by
SMALL WORLD BIG DREAMS

Artist Sara Clement created this wall in both English and German outside her art studio in Berlin. "What I really liked about the wall is that there was such a variety of answers, from silly ones to profound ones," she said. "That was the great thing about it, the freedom to write whatever you wanted." She shared some of the most memorable moments for her. "A man passing by stopped and, with a grin, he wrote 'erdbeer-torte essen' (eat strawberry cake) as he was off to the café next door. Had it not been for the wall, we wouldn't have interacted with him." The best part of the day, she said, was when a group of kids came along. "I handed them a box of chalk and they went wild drawing on the board: hearts, stars and rainbows — imagery that was hopeful and full of life. They were really enjoying the moment, which is something that as adults we need to remind ourselves: enjoy the now."

made with love by SARAH CLEMENT, OCEANYAM, AND FRANK DYBALLA

Before I die I want to...

build stuff.

Before I die I want to...

reach my constant happiness.

Before I die I want to...

eat strawberry cake.

Before I die I want to...

be a famous artist.

Before I die I want to...

own a small pig.

Sarah Clement

Before I die I want to
WUNDER
Before I die I want to
Before I die I want to
Before I die I want to
HAVE A BABY
Before I die I want to
WATCH MY SON FALL IN LOVE
Be truthful to me & others
Before I die I want to
FALL IN LOVE 4 REAL
Forgive
Before I die I want to
I SEE MY SOUL IN YOUR EYES
Before I die I want to
BE LOVED
Before I die I want to
EXPERIENCE AS MUCH AS I CAN
I WANT TO LIVE MY LIFE THE FULLEST
KNOW MY DAUGHTER IS OKAY

Mark Hammon

EXISTS ONLY ONE WEEK A YEAR DURING THE BURNING MAN FESTIVAL
AFTER THE FESTIVAL, THE SITE IS A STARK WHITE DESERT
POPULATION: 0

Black Rock City
Nevada

organized by
BURNING MAN

Every September, tens of thousands of people gather in the middle of Nevada's Great Basin for the famed Burning Man festival. Thanks to the organizers, a Before I Die wall appeared among the crowds. "So many interesting things were written and I hated washing them off when the wall filled up," said artist Susan Moore, who installed the wall. "Space travel seemed to be a popular theme, but I think my favorite was simply, 'Before I die I want to find my sleeping bag.'" The responses ranged from the whimsical and comic to the personal and heartfelt. Burning Man volunteer Marty Marks had quadruple bypass coronary artery surgery before the festival. "That was the closest thing to dying that I had ever experienced," he said. "So for me, it was particularly appropriate to be the first one to scrawl on the wall. I wrote, 'Before I die I want to come back to Burning Man!'"

made with love by SUSAN MOORE, LISA GORMAN, RICHARD JOHNSON, AND MARIA PARTRIDGE WITH SUPPORT FROM THE BLACK ROCK ARTS FOUNDATION

Before I die I want to...

support myself with my art.

Mark Hammon

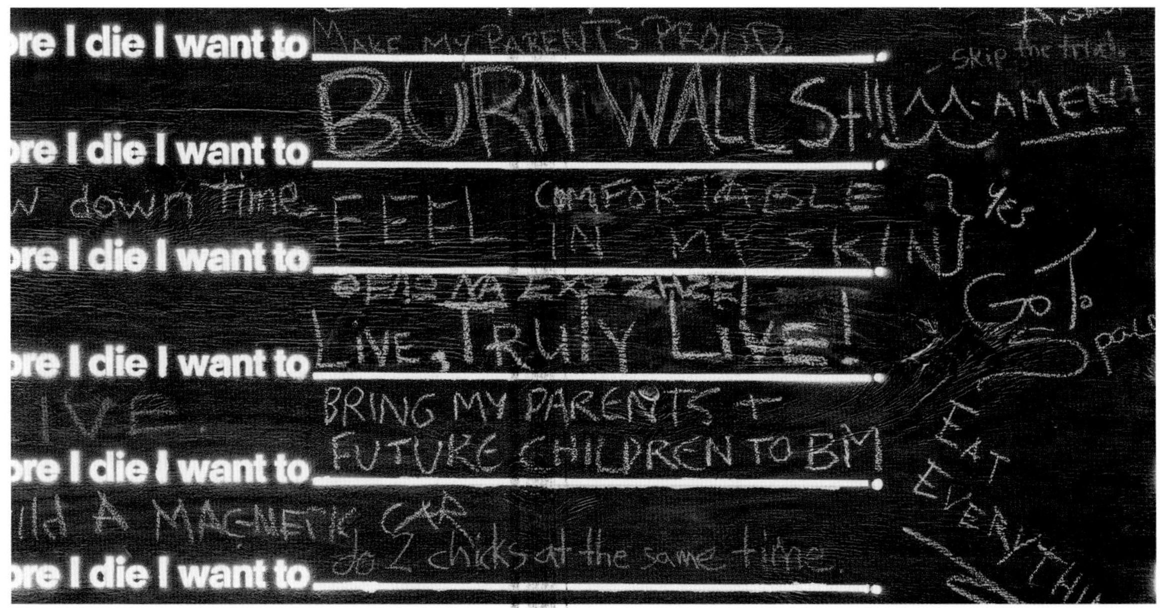

Before I die I want to...

find my sleeping bag.

Before I die I want to...

feel comfortable in my skin.

Before I die I want to...

build a magnetic car

Before I die I want to...

have no regrets.

BLOOMBERG
INTEGRATE
NYC
FEATHERED
LOTTO!
BE The
next OPRAH
GROW
OCCUPY
I want to
ENJOY LIFE
I want to
Go Back to School
I want to
I want to
I want to
BUY MOM A HOUSE
I want to
I want to
pie
meet my
HAVE A
WORLD

Jeff Scher

CONEY ISLAND IS HOME TO THE FIRST ROLLERCOASTER IN AMERICA
BIRTHPLACE OF GEORGE GERSHWIN, LOU REED, AND FAB FIVE FREDDY
POPULATION: 2.6 MILLION

Brooklyn

New York

organized by
SHAKE SHACK

Blue construction barriers are almost as common as pigeons in New York City. Many of them are blank or plastered with ads. As the restaurant Shake Shack built a new storefront in the heart of downtown Brooklyn, their generous team turned their barriers into a constructive place for the community — and one of the longest Before I Die walls ever. I used to live a few blocks from the area so I was extra excited to read responses from afar and get to know my old neighbors in new ways. Theresa Mullen, who spearheaded the installation, shared stories of how the wall unfolded over its three-month life. "Hardly anyone writes anymore, so it was especially poignant to see all this sharing with the written word," she said. "I watched a woman stand for a long time, reading, smiling, thinking. She finally wrote 'Find God' in small words and started crying. All of this sharing amongst total strangers in such a heavily trafficked location was breathtaking."

made with love by THERESA MULLEN, ANDREW MCCAUGHAN, JESSICA ROTHSCHILD, MIKE TUIACH, KEVIN SCHWARTZ, MOE FOY, LACE ABEL-BEY, REBECCA HASTINGS, STEPHEN PIRMAL, TOM HIRO, AND SHAWMUT DESIGN AND CONSTRUCTION TEAM

Shake Shack

Before I die I want to...

be someone's favorite.

Before I die I want to...

live without fearing death.

Before I die I want to...

bring peace of mind to my mom.

Belinda Kanpetch

Before I die...
Before I die I want to
Before I die I want to
Before I die I want to
Before I die I want to
Before I die I want to
Before I die I want to
Before I die I want to
BEFORE I DIE I WANT TO EARN A
BEFORE I DIE,
I WANT TO CLIMB
MOUNT EVEREST!

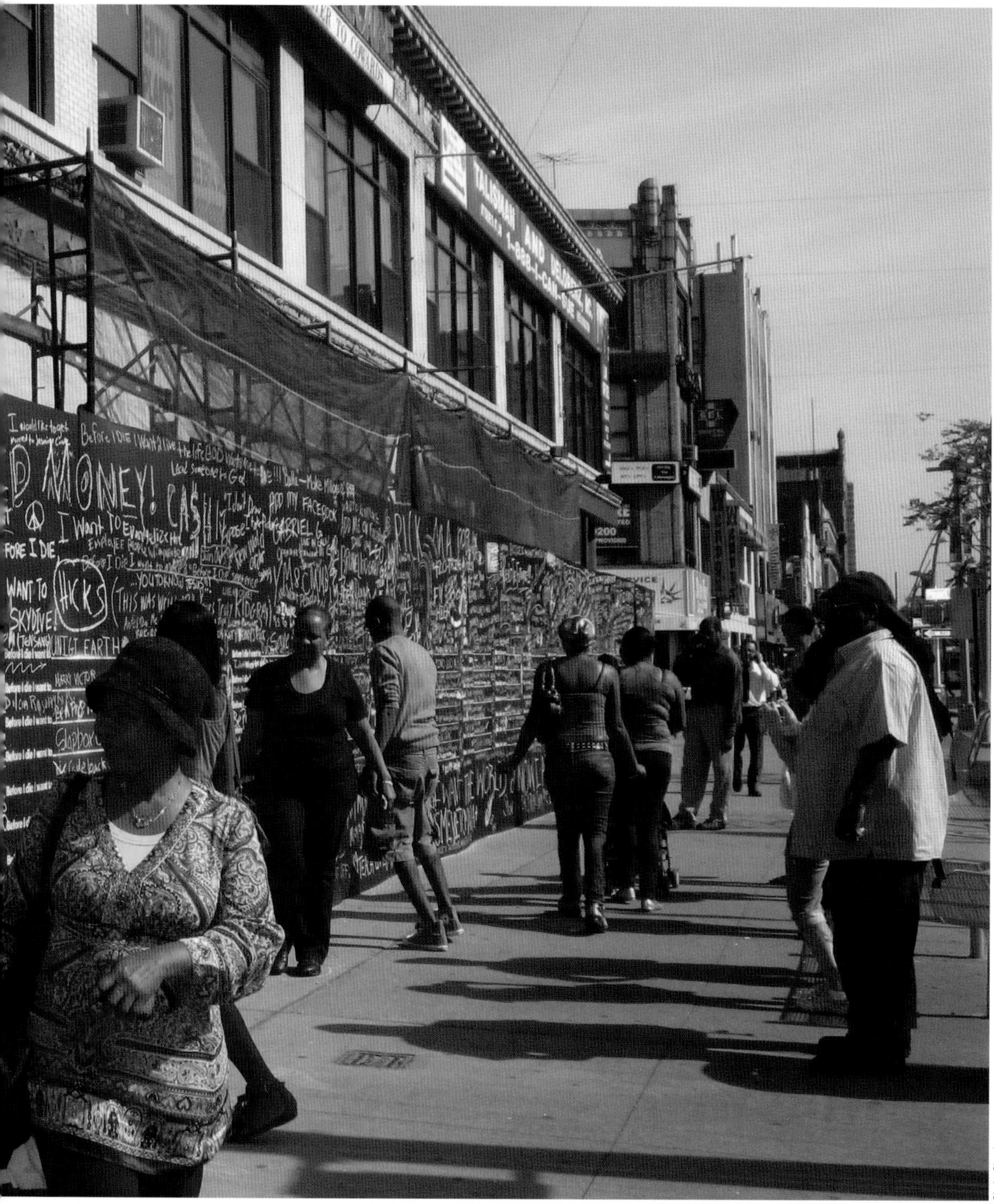

Shake Shack

Before I die I want to...

lose this damn weight.

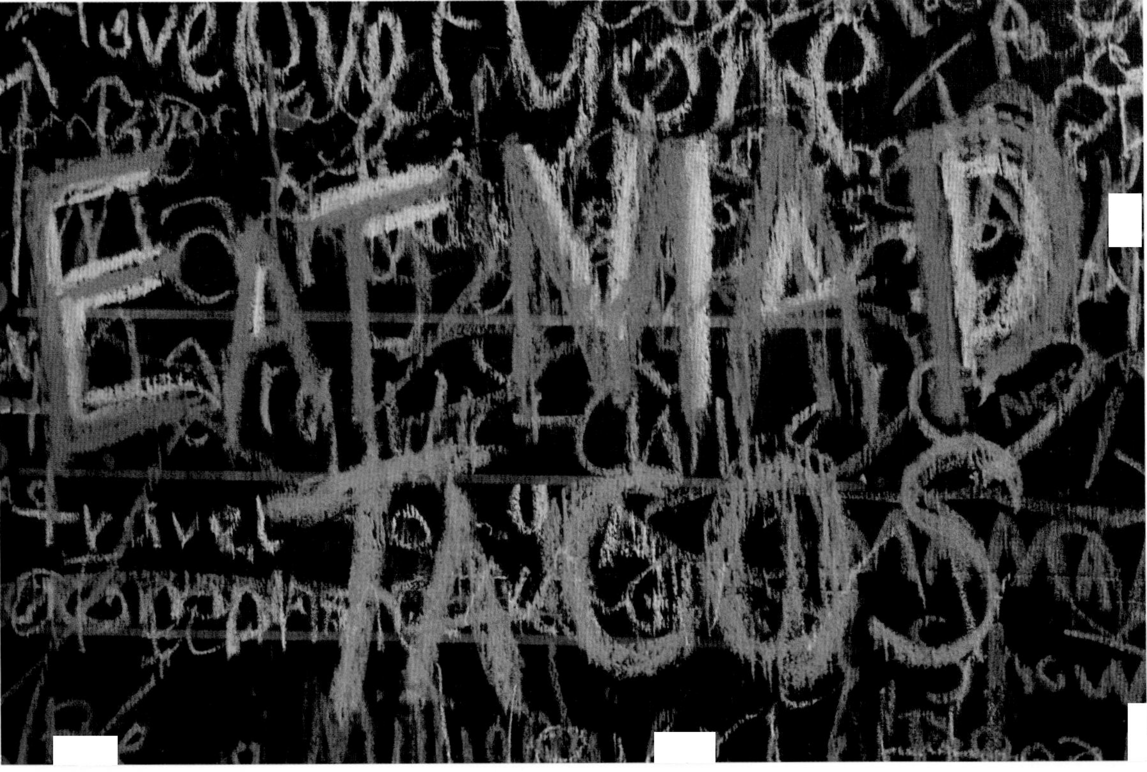

Victor Hu

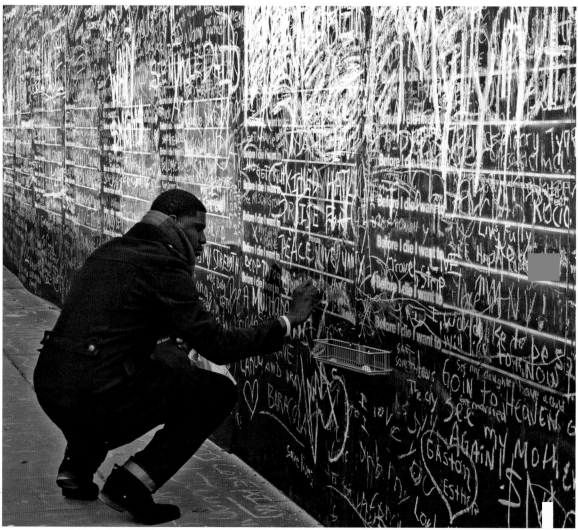

Belinda Kanpetch

Before I die I want to...

pay my student loans.

Before I die I want to...

get an 'A' in math.

Steven Slotow

Colette Weintraub

HAS A THRIVING PENGUIN COLONY
FIRST HUMAN HEART TRANSPLANT IN THE WORLD PERFORMED HERE IN 1967
POPULATION: 3.4 MILLION

Cape Town

South Africa

organized by
ELENA IOULIANOU & STEVEN SLOTOW

After building a Before I Die wall in Johannesburg, Steven Slotow flew down to Cape Town to help organize a wall on Long Street. "Packed full of bars, night clubs, restaurants, and the best milkshakes in the Southern hemisphere, it's where you start," he said. Getting permission from the city, however, wasn't easy. "This became quite apparent as we quickly got the door slammed in our face for one reason: council approval. Apparently even the owner of a property can't give permission to do something on the outside of his house without council approval." Then a friend connected him with the Unknown Union, a street art shop, and they offered their wall as a canvas, no council approval needed. "We picked up a few hangers-on who helped out and did a lot of drawing on the street in chalk. And I wrote the same thing on the wall that I did in Johannesburg: 'I'm already doing it!'"

made with love by ELENA IOULIANOU, SIMEON SPIERINGSHOEK, CHRIS MASON, ATHENA LAMBERIS, RICHARD SEPTEMBER, AND GUBZIN THOLE

Disprove Religion
FIND THE CURE!
I WANT TO SAVE ALL THE ANIMALS
Before I Die I want to star in a parade
* WRITE A BOOK
Before I Die I want to Swim w/ the
FINISH WHAT I STARTED.
Before I Die I want to Tell the Universe THANKS!
Before I Die I want to Go all around the world
Before I Die I want to Kiss Princeston
Before I Die I want to BUY TESS 1, 2, 3 SHOTS
Before I Die I want to GRADUATE COLLEGE
Before I Die I want to PLAY ON LETTERMAN
Before I Die I want to Have DONE Everything I was MeANT TO
Before I Die I want to FIND LOVE (true)
Before I Die I want to EVACUATE ON THE U.N.
LIVE
HIKE THE APPALACHIAN TRAIL

Nicole Diefenbach

HOLDS THE LARGEST OYSTER FESTIVAL IN THE WORLD
NAMED THE MOST POLITE CITY IN AMERICA
POPULATION: 122,689

Charleston
South Carolina

organized by
REDUX STUDIOS

This wall was installed on the side of Redux Studios, a community art center in historic downtown Charleston, thanks to local newspaper ad exec Nicole Diefenbach. The center offered their wall as a canvas and the city paper donated all the paint, brushes, and chalk. Nicole and ten of her friends spent two weekends setting it up, stenciling 106 prompts until one in the morning the night before the installation opened. People drove from as far as three hours away to write on the wall, which collected responses from "run through flowers in the Swiss Alps" to "stop thinking and do it." "Charleston is a friendly community," said Nicole. "Strangers would stand around talking about what they were writing and why. It really brought them together. A young woman pushing a baby carriage stopped to write, 'I want to meet my grandkids.' I was really touched."

made with love by NICOLE DIEFENBACH, ANDREW PAPPAS, DREW FUZY, DAVID USI, KELSEY DUNN, AND LANDON PHILLIPS

Before I die I want to...

light a car on fire and watch it burn.

Before I die I want to...

take a sculpting class.

Before I die I want to...

run through flowers in the Swiss Alps.

Before I die I want to...

collect folk knowledge.

Before I die I want to...

stop thinking and do it.

Before I die I want to...

create a masterpiece.

Vin Threeprom

NICKNAMED THE ROSE OF THE NORTH
THOUSANDS OF PAPER LANTERNS ARE RELEASED AT THE FESTIVAL OF LIGHTS
POPULATION: 146,346

Chiang Mai

Thailand

organized by
BAR FRY

When Vin Threeprom opened his french fry shop Bar Fry in Chiang Mai, he imagined it as more than a restaurant. "I also want it to be an open art space for people to meet and hang around." For three months he wrapped the fill-in-the-blank sentence along the walls of his space and on the counter. "In the first week not many customers had the courage to write anything on the wall. But in the coming weeks, the wall was so filled it was about to explode. It was too much, and it got really funny." Responses ranged from "ride a horse on Inner Mongolia prairies" to "warp students' minds" to "ride my bike up the top ten highest mountains in Thailand." And someone else, while assumingly eating some delicious fries, wrote "buff up."

made with love by VIN THREEPROM

Before I die I want to ________________

Before I die I want to ________________

Before I die I want to ________________

Before I die I want to ________________

Before I die I want to ________________

Before I die I want to ________________

Before I die I want to ________________

Elizabeth Shank

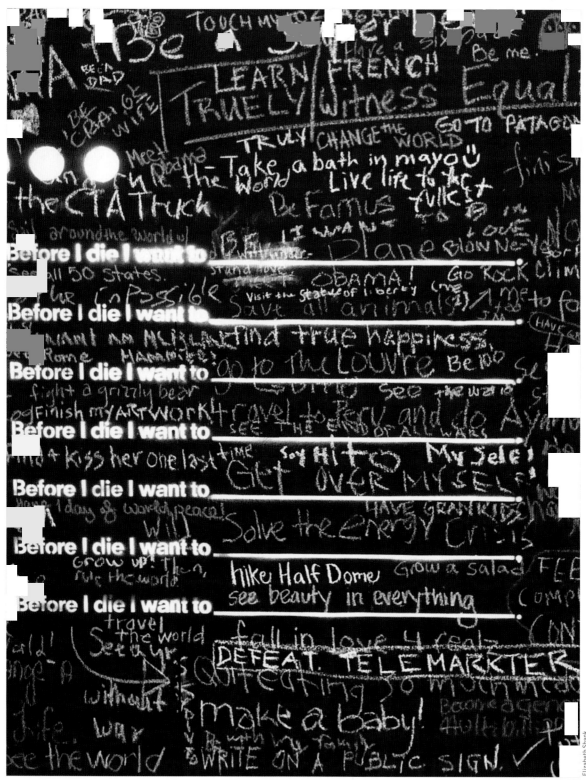

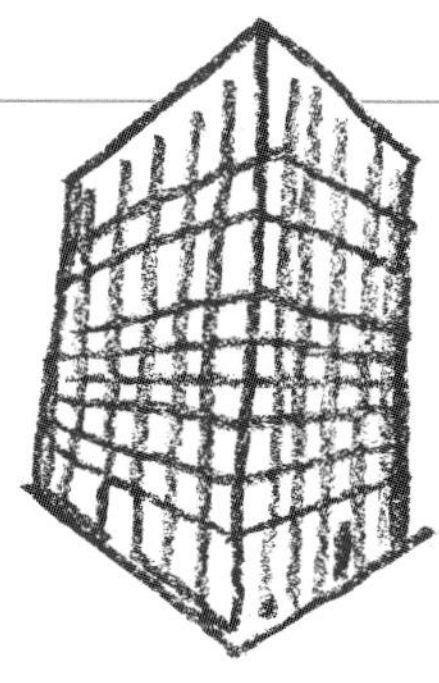

BIRTHPLACE OF THE SKYSCRAPER
THE FIRST FERRIS WHEEL WAS BUILT HERE
POPULATION: 2.7 MILLION

Chicago
Illinois

organized by
GOOD NEWS ONLY & CHICAGO URBAN ART SOCIETY

Five walls emerged in neighborhoods across Chicago thanks in part to Good News Only, a non-profit gallery that teaches local youth how to manage a fine art gallery and develop art exhibitions. Students, local residents, and even politicians and building owners helped paint and stencil the walls, and Rust-Oleum donated paint. "The walls brought many different people from the community to a single location, where they stood together to simply read or write or they actually discussed the remarks on the wall," said Elizabeth Shank, founder of Good News Only. "When we were installing the first site, a neighbor came by to watch, and as we were peeling the stencils off, she grabbed some chalk and wrote 'Forgive and be forgiven.' She stood and stared at her words, not showing any urgency to walk away — almost like she was protecting them. I could just imagine the cathartic moment she was having. It was very powerful."

made with love by CHICAGO URBAN ART SOCIETY, GOOD NEWS ONLY, RUST-OLEUM, TAE HWAN HAN, YOLLOCALLI YOUTH ARTS REACH, ALDERMAN DANIEL SOLIS, LITTLE VILLAGE CHAMBER OF COMMERCE, UNIVERSIDAD POPULAR, AND LILLSTREET ART CENTER

Elizabeth Shank

Before I die I want to...

see a year without war.

Before I die I want to...

grow a salad.

Before I die I want to...

receive my citizenship.

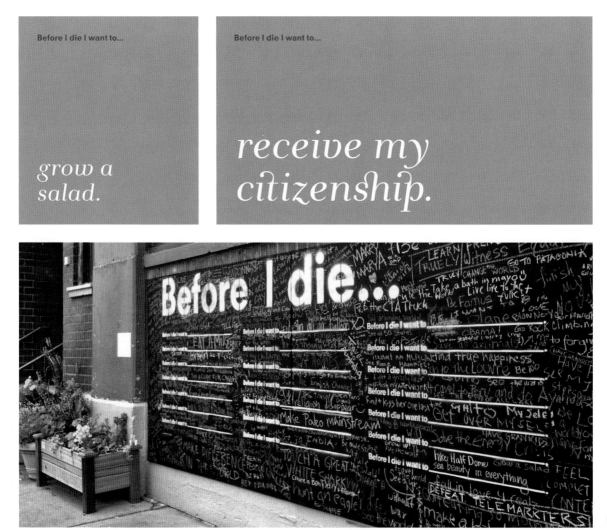

Before I die I want to...

meet my neighbors.

Before I die I want to...

find and kiss her one last time.

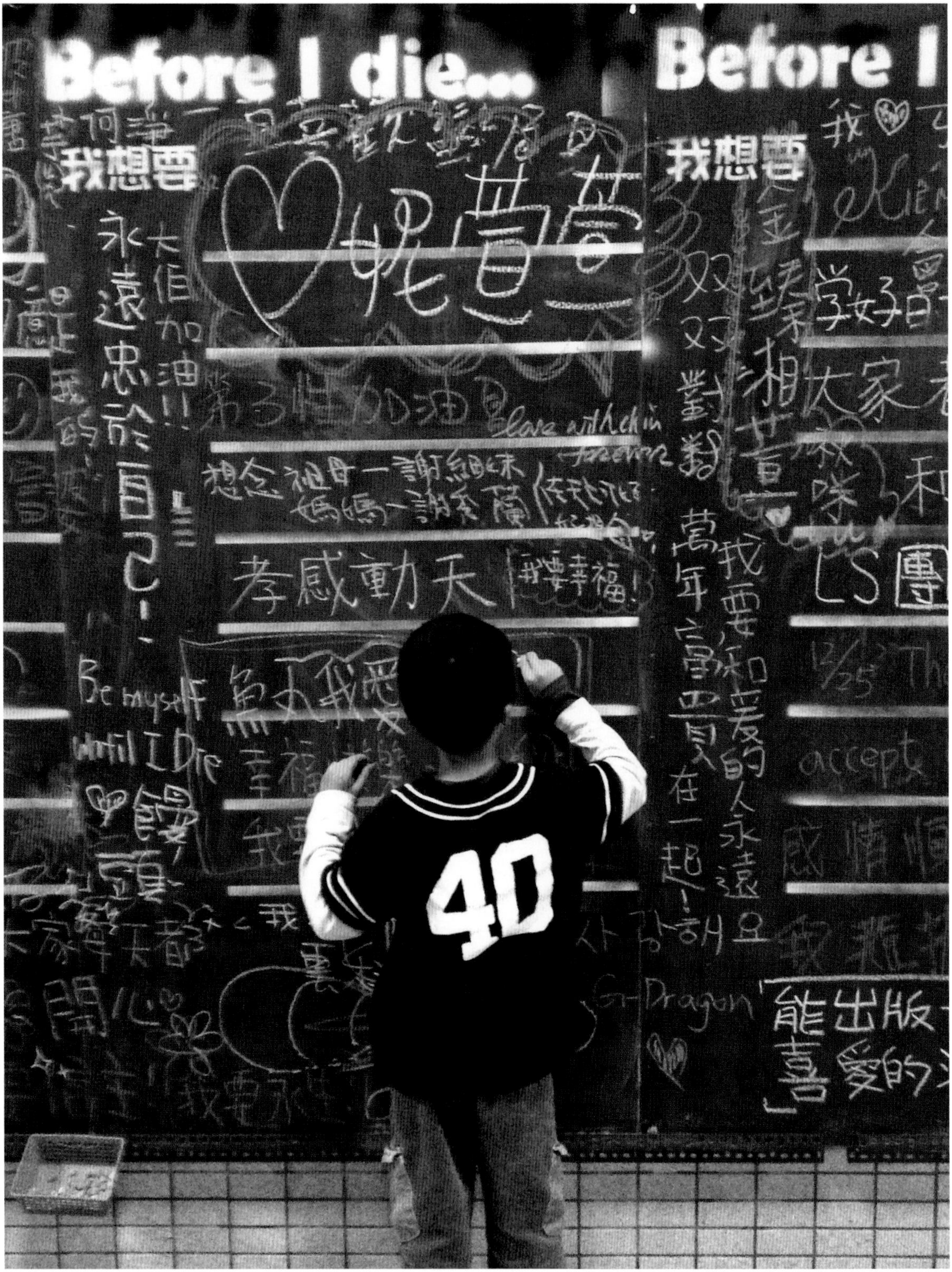

Sammy Tsao

NEAR THE HISTORIC WHITE SAND CAPE LIGHT HOUSE
HAS A SOFT DRINK MUSEUM
POPULATION: 369,770

Chung-Li
Taiwan

organized by
CHUNG-LI PRESBYTERIAN CHURCH

My parents are from Taiwan so I was happy to hear about this wall and even happier to hear about the response to it. When deacon En Ron "Sammy" Tsao decided to create a wall at his church, he wasn't sure what to expect. "Taiwanese society is very sensitive when it comes to talking about death and avoids it like a taboo. I decided to write the words 'Before I die' in English and then use Chinese for the rest of the sentence." To his surprise, people filled the boards before volunteers could finish installing it. Sammy estimates 25,000 people have written on the boards over the five months it's been up so far. "Some people became curious about the church as well and began attending services. The influx of people to the area also boosted business for nearby stores. Some store owners said they hope we will add more blackboards!"

made with love by MARV TSAO, MR.CHOU, AND EN RON TSAO

Sammy Tsao

Before I die I want to...

apologize to you.

Before I die I want to...

keep getting better every day.

Before I die I want to...

ride a bike around this island.

Before I die I want to...

have a big garden with flowers in bloom.

Before I die I want to...

be an Olympic champion.

Jenny Carden

ITS MOUNTAINS ARE KNOWN FOR UFO SIGHTINGS
HOSTS AN ANNUAL CHOCOLATE FESTIVAL
POPULATION: 1.4 MILLION

Córdoba
Argentina

organized by
JENNY CARDEN & FRIENDS

Near the center of Argentina lies Córdoba, the second largest city in the country. On a crisp day in May, Jenny Carden and her friends added a layer of chalkboard paint to a regularly graffitied wall and turned it into one of the most stunning walls I've seen. "In less than 26 hours of spraying the last stencil, there was not a bare inch of wall remaining," said Jenny. "It was one thing to see the Before I Die project on my computer screen and quite another to see it in action. I had no idea it would have such a powerful effect on such a wide range of people. People in South America live at a slower pace and almost everyone stopped to read the wall: old men with briefcases, couples on walks, kids running home from school. I think everyone loved that they were being invited to make their mark on the wall. They say the first thing you need to do to make your big desires come true in life is to write them down."

made with love by JENNY CARDEN, NESTOR BUSTAMANTE, LUCAS CARO, JULIANNA CARO, DAMIAN LINOSSI, ELINA MARUCCI, FEDE MORILLA, GABRIEL MURUAGA, MAGDALENA RUIZ, AND SASHA VOROBYOVA

Before I die I want to...

compose a beautiful song.

Before I die I want to...

love and be loved.

(l) Jenny Carden (r) Damion Linossi

Before I die I want to...

speak more than ten languages.

Jenny Carden

Antes de
Antes de morir quiero
SER FELIZ
Antes de morir quiero
TENER UN HIJO
ENSEÑAR CON PASION
Antes de morir quiero
Antes de morir quiero
ESCRIBIR UN LIBRO.
Antes de morir quiero
VIAJAR
Antes de morir quiero
Antes de morir quiero
Antes de morir quiero
Antes de morir quiero
APRENDER DE MIS ERRORES!
Antes de morir quiero
Antes de morir quiero
Antes de morir quiero
SER ACTRIZ
COMER ROSQUITAS

Jenny Carden

Damion Linossi

Before I die I want to...

learn to get on a stage.

Before I die I want to...

open my own restaurant.

Before I die I want to...

speak with my children one last time.

Before I die...

قبل أن أموت...

SocialBandage, Ataya, Startup Weekend Dubai, Startup Weekend Abu Dhabi

CAMEL POLO IS PLAYED HERE
HOME OF THE TALLEST SKYSCRAPER IN THE WORLD
POPULATION: 2.1 MILLION

Dubai

United Arab Emirates

organized by
SOCIALBANDAGE

After Aisha Harib's mother passed away from cancer that was discovered very late, she founded Social Bandage, an organization that raises awareness for people in need of medical help. Social Bandage installed Before I Die walls in English and Arabic at a charity art exhibition to raise funds for children with cancer. During the month of May, the walls filled with hopes to "go to space," "skydive successfully," "be a part of this great country," "save lives," and "become the next Mother Theresa." The organization continued the experiment at similar events in Abu Dhabi. "We created those walls to motivate and inspire others," said Aisha, "and to raise awareness of our shared humanity."

Made with love by SOCIALBANDAGE, ATAYA, STARTUP WEEKEND DUBAI, AND STARTUP WEEKEND ABU DHABI

Jennifer Muldowney

THE REMAINS OF ST. VALENTINE REST HERE
BIRTHPLACE OF JAMES JOYCE, OSCAR WILDE AND BRAM STOKER
POPULATION: 1.2 MILLION

Dublin
Ireland

organized by
ELEPHANT IN THE ROOM

This wall was installed at the Over 50s Show in Dublin as part of the Elephant in the Room stand, an end-of-life planning project organized by a funeral planner, a financial advisor, and a solicitor. "The objective was to get people to start thinking ahead and preplanning, but it's such a grim subject," said Jennifer Muldowney, the funeral planner of the group. "When we came across the Before I Die project, we thought it would be appropriate to get people over fifty thinking about their life, achievements, hopes for the future, dreams, and ultimate bucket list." Responses included "learn to paint," "fall in love," "get married for the 10th time," and "ride a bike in the nude." "And a 78-year-old nun who wanted to finish her degree!" said Jennifer. "There were queues to take the chalk. What was surprising was how many of the wishes were achievable but hadn't yet been achieved."

made with love by JENNIFER MULDOWNEY, GERRY MULDOWNEY, AND JOANNE SMITH

Burkhard Gruess

EUROPE'S LARGEST VEGETABLE SEED PRODUCER
ITS TOWN SQUARE IS A PRESERVED MEDIEVAL TOWN
POPULATION: 200,000

Erfurt *Germany*

organized by
BURKHARD GRUESS & FLORIAN ORTLOFF

"Erfurt, as a city, is gaining interest in public art and we wanted to see how our community of students and blue-collar workers would interact with the wall," said Burkhard Gruess who, with Florian Ortloff, built an impressive freestanding wall on a vacant lot in their neighborhood. Simple universal wishes sat next to to more mysterious ones. "The responses that most caught our attention were wishes like 'I want to see my parents again' or 'I want to talk to Friedhelm.' These kinds of wishes make you wonder about the story behind them. What kind of tragedy and fate occurred to the people involved?" The wall had other side effects too. "The great thing about this project is Florian and I both realized that you can make a difference in your community. Now we're thinking about doing another project together. Because of this one, I told myself, 'come on, just try it out, even if it doesn´t work.'"

made with love by BURKHARD GRUESS & FLORIAN ORTLOFF. SUPPORTED BY THINK BIG, LADEBALKEN E.V., BÜRGERBEIRAT ILVERGEHOFEN, BENE NUETZEL AND KLANGGERÜST E.V.

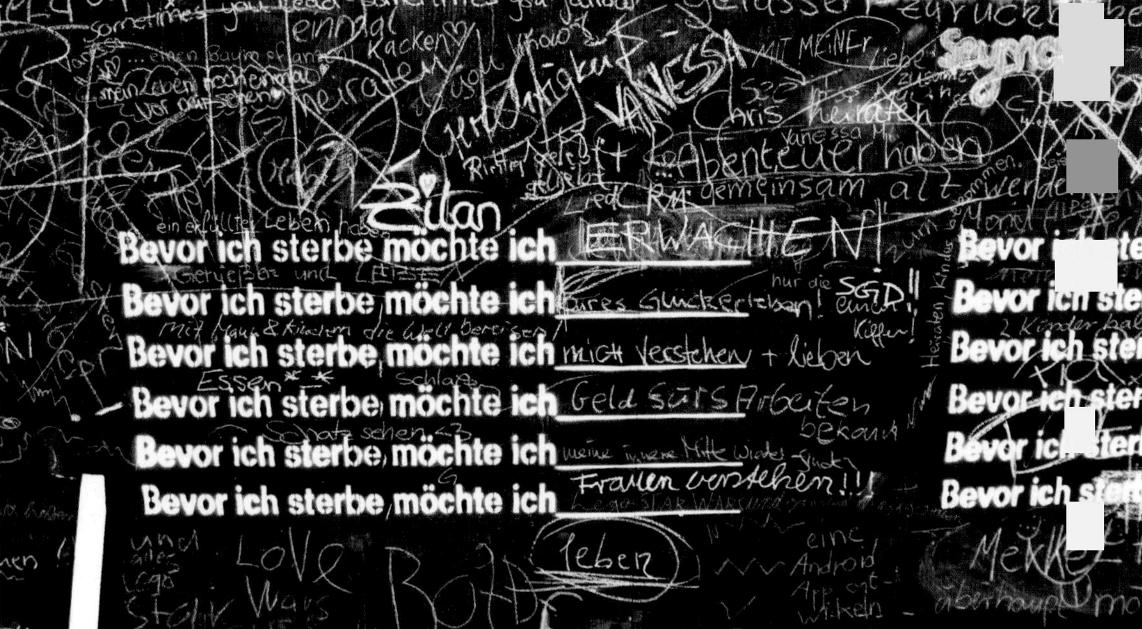

Burkhard Gruess

Before I die I want to...

plant a tree.

Before I die I want to...

find closure.

Before I die I want to...

understand women.

Before I die I want to...

have a good day.

Before I die I want to...

see my parents again.

Before I die I want to...

chase a tornado.

HOLLY'S STORY

My best friend and I were on holiday in Jamaica and a storm whipped up on the sea with visible tornados in the distance. I can only say, being fourteen at the time, it was my most exhiliarating experience to date. Heart like a hummingbird and eyes in wonder. Nature is extradordinary in its immensity and its power to destroy and change the face of the earth. I think the experience stuck with me because it's one I associate with being deliriously happy — the kind of happy where you just want to laugh and cry at the same time.

As friends tend to do, we make crazy plans, pinky promise it's a deal, forget them, and make new ones. But now my friend and I made a list. It's personal to us and currently pinned on her board. In some ways it's like having our own wall and who knows if we'll achieve them, but the list is about the journey and the memories we'll bring back about the time we storm-chased a tornado.

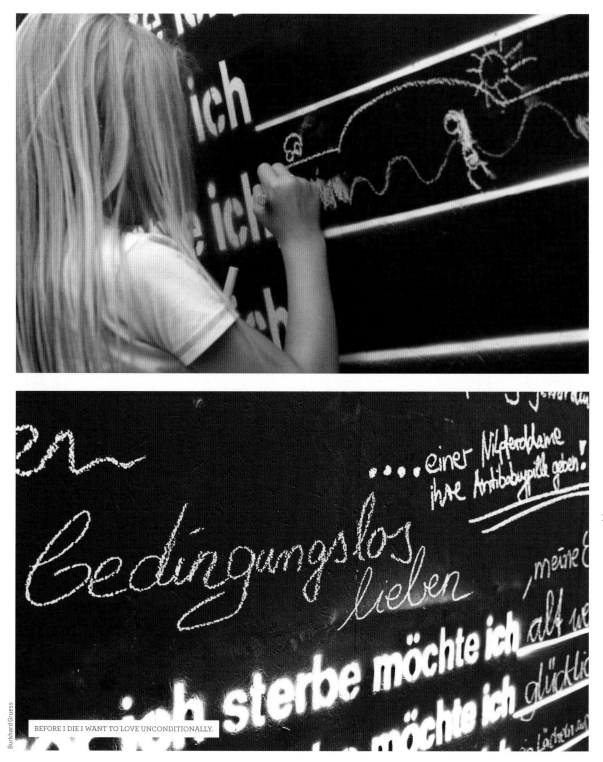

BEFORE I DIE I WANT TO LOVE UNCONDITIONALLY.

Burkhard Gruess

Swapna Gangadharan

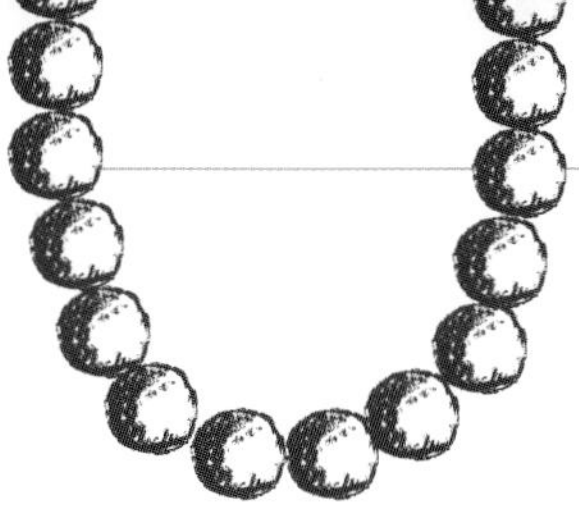

KNOWN AS THE CITY OF PEARLS
IT IS NESTLED AMONG 2.5 BILLION YEAR OLD ROCK FORMATIONS
POPULATION: 6.8 MILLION

Hyderabad
India

organized by
TRUFFLES CAFE

Alongside the explosive growth of technology, infrastructure, education, and consumer goods in India, café-owner Swapna Gangadharan noticed a side effect of the rapid change. "With luxuries came the desire to go more for external things rather than look at oneself internally, and this is growing at an alarming rate in younger generations," she said. "We believe that in spite of all that, there is this 'chip' inside everyone, a chip of sensitivity towards our surroundings, environments, and issues that people do care about, but they have just gone off track." With help from her partner and local artists, Swapna installed the wall on the entrance to her café, where responses ranged from "take care of my parents" to "travel across India on a bike" to the more humble "bake bread."

made with love by RAJIV NAIR AND HIS TEAM

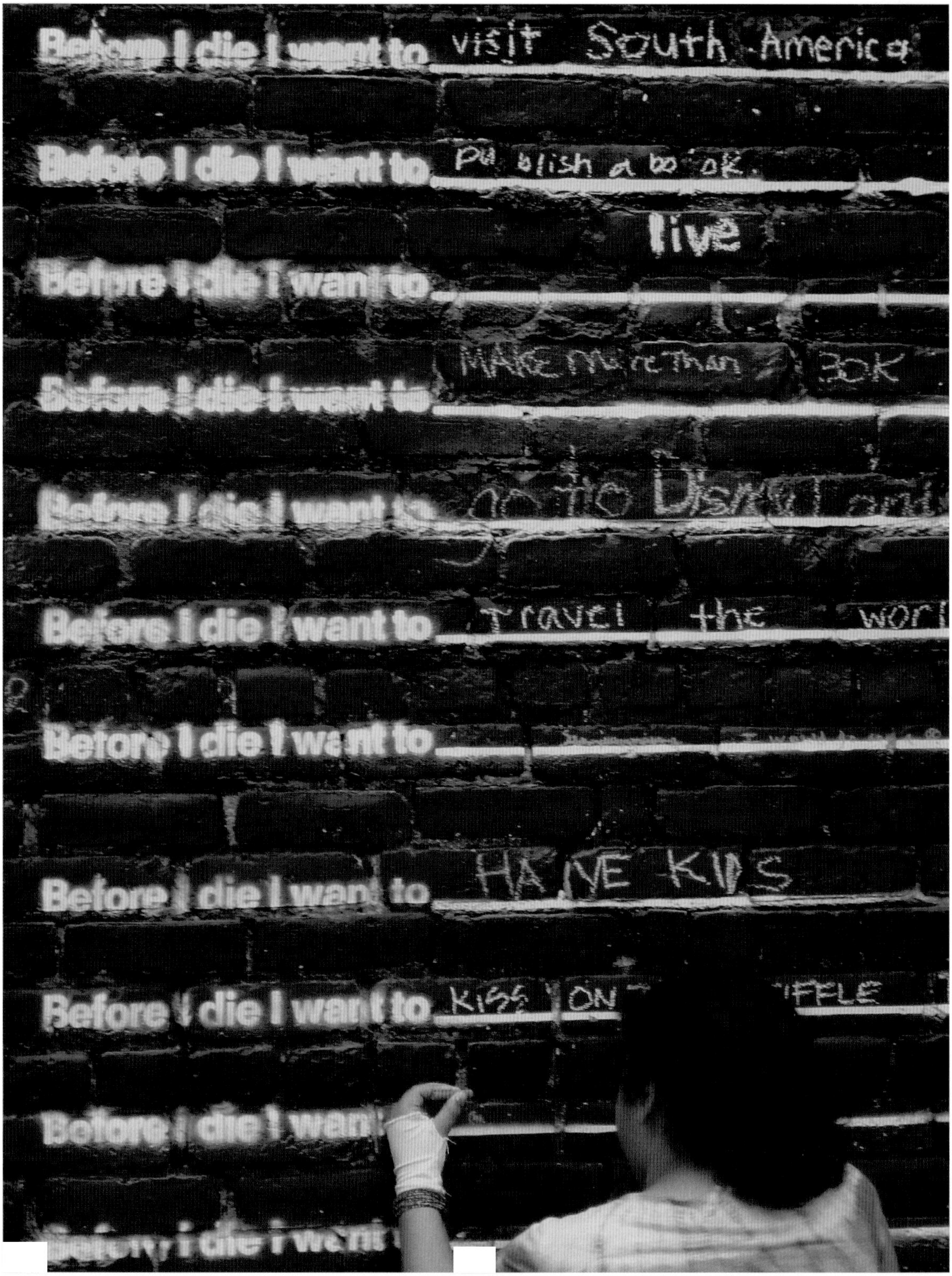

Deirdre Murphy

SITE OF THE FIRST SKYWAY HIGHWAY EVER BUILT
THE STATUE OF LIBERTY IS ONLY 2,000 FEET FROM ITS SHORE
POPULATION: 250,323

Jersey City
New Jersey

organized by
SMALL WORLD BIG DREAMS

Thanks to the organizational prowess of four friends in four corners of the world, walls went up in Jersey City, Berlin, Vancouver, and Townsville, Australia, at the same time (all of which are featured in this book). Dierdre Murphy installed this wall in Jersey City behind an abandoned building. The day it went up, the vacant lot across the street was transformed into the temporary stage for a chili cook-off. Live music played and people drifted back and forth between eating chili and talking about the wall, which collected desires to "drive on the Autobahn," "learn Chinese," "start my own business," and "go to Disneyworld." "A few of us noticed how simple some of the dreams were," said Deirdre. "They seemed totally attainable — things people could do very easily. It was fascinating to realize that everyone sees different limitations and different possibilities in their lives."

made with love by DEIRDRE MURPHY AND JESÚS DÍEZ GARCÍA WITH THE HELP OF FOURTH STREET ARTS

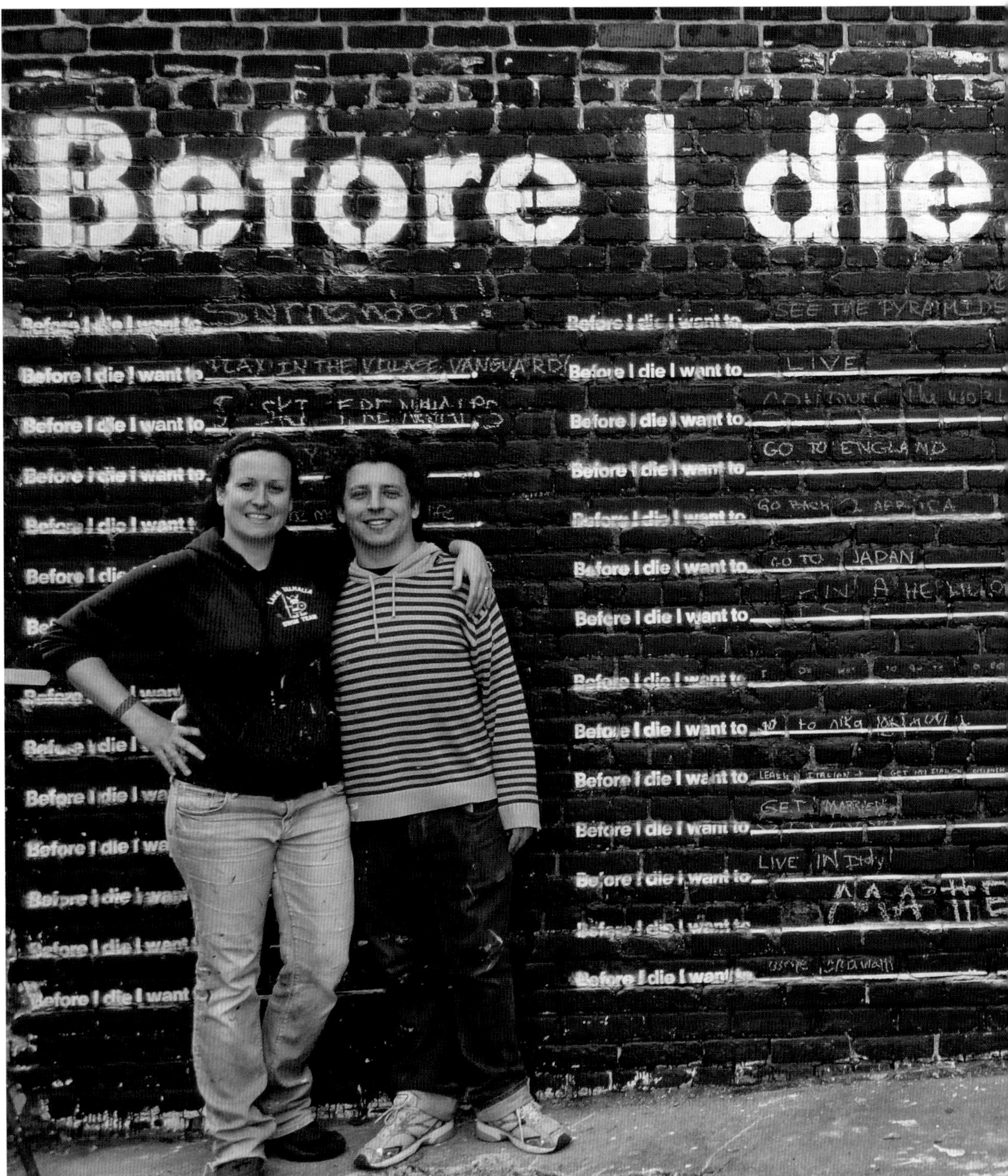
Before I die
Before I die I want to SURRENDER
Before I die I want to SEE THE PYRAMIDS
Before I die I want to PLAY IN THE VILLAGE VANGUARD!
Before I die I want to LIVE
Before I die I want to
GO TO ENGLAND
Before I die I want to
GO BACK 2 AFRICA
Before I die I want to GO TO JAPAN
Before I die I want to
Before I die I want to
Before I die I want to
Before I die I want to LEARN ITALIAN
GET MARRIED
Before I die I want to
LIVE IN Italy
Before I die I want to

DIERDRE MURPHY AND HER HUSBAND JESUS DÍEZ GARCÍA

Kevin Murphy

Before I die I want to...

kiss on the top of the Eiffel Tower.

Before I die I want to...

build a theater.

Deirdre Murphy

Deirdre Murphy

Before I die I want to...

create like crazy.

Before I die I want to...

be my own boss.

Before I die I want to...

win a grappling tournament.

TEDxJerusalem

HOME OF THE OLDEST ACTIVE CEMETERY, THE MOUNT OF OLIVES
THE CITY IS MENTIONED OVER 700 TIMES IN THE BIBLE
POPULATION: 768,000

Jerusalem
Israel

organized by
TEDXJERUSALEM

This wall was installed by TEDxJerusalem as part of their conference at the Jerusalem YMCA. "The location was extremely important to us since it represented a place where we can put aside our differences and concentrate on sharing ideas and experiences that connect us," explained Beto Maya, who organized the project. "The team dedicated this wall to the artist Azriel Cohen, who passed away in his sleep a few months before the event." Across the top of the board, Cohen is described as an "artist, visionary, healer, mystical renaissance man, and true friend of Jerusalem." With responses such as "write a piano concerto," "be myself around others as I am by myself," "appreciate now," "stop being afraid," "live to the fullest," and "feel unity in Jerusalem," hopefully this wall captured some of his spirit.

made with love by MICHALYA SCHONWALD MOSS, ANJA WALESON, BETO MAYA, BRACHIE SPRUNG, HANEEN MAGADLH, IDO LEVIT, LIRON ZABARI, SIVAN VARDI, FAZA HEART & MIND MARKETING, AND SAY

Steven Slotow

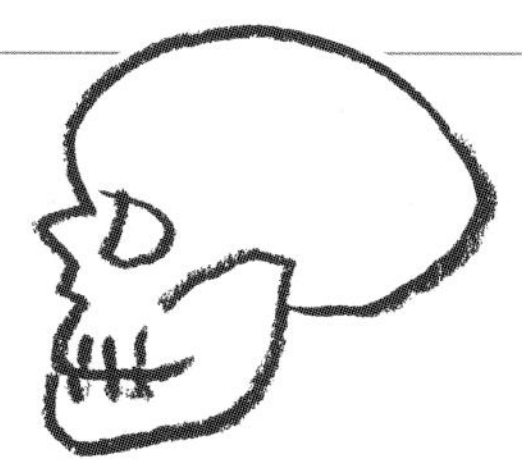

40% OF THE PLANET'S HUMAN ANCESTOR FOSSILS WERE DISCOVERED HERE
HAS THE WORLD'S BIGGEST MAN-MADE FOREST, WITH OVER 10 MILLION TREES
POPULATION: 3.2 MILLION

Johannesburg
South Africa

organized by
STEVEN SLOTOW

Johannesburg has had a special place in my heart ever since I worked there a few years ago, so I was delighted when Steven Slotow, a local writer, said he was organizing a wall. He found a choice spot in the Maboneng Precinct, a cultural hub in the city center known for its mix of galleries, artist studios, and creative venues. He teamed up with artists who framed the wall with their own great works, and they unveiled the wall during the Urban Arts Festival. "We got done stenciling early, but it wasn't early enough," Steven said. "Before the white spray paint could dry, visitors of the popular Maboneng flea market were flocking to the wall to share their dreams. I visited each Sunday morning to jot down the old dreams and wipe it down to make space for the new ones. I was never disappointed."

made with love by STEVEN SLOTOW, ELENA IOULIANOU, SIMEON SPIERINGSHOEK, CHRIS MASON, ATHENA LAMBERIS, RICHARD SEPTEMBER, AND GUBZIN THOLE

Before I die I want to...

swim in a pile of autumn leaves.

Before I die I want to...

master the trumpet.

Before I die I want to...

have my own theme song.

Steven Slotow

Before I die I want to...

teach kids to live, love, and be free.

Before I die I want to...

help out more.

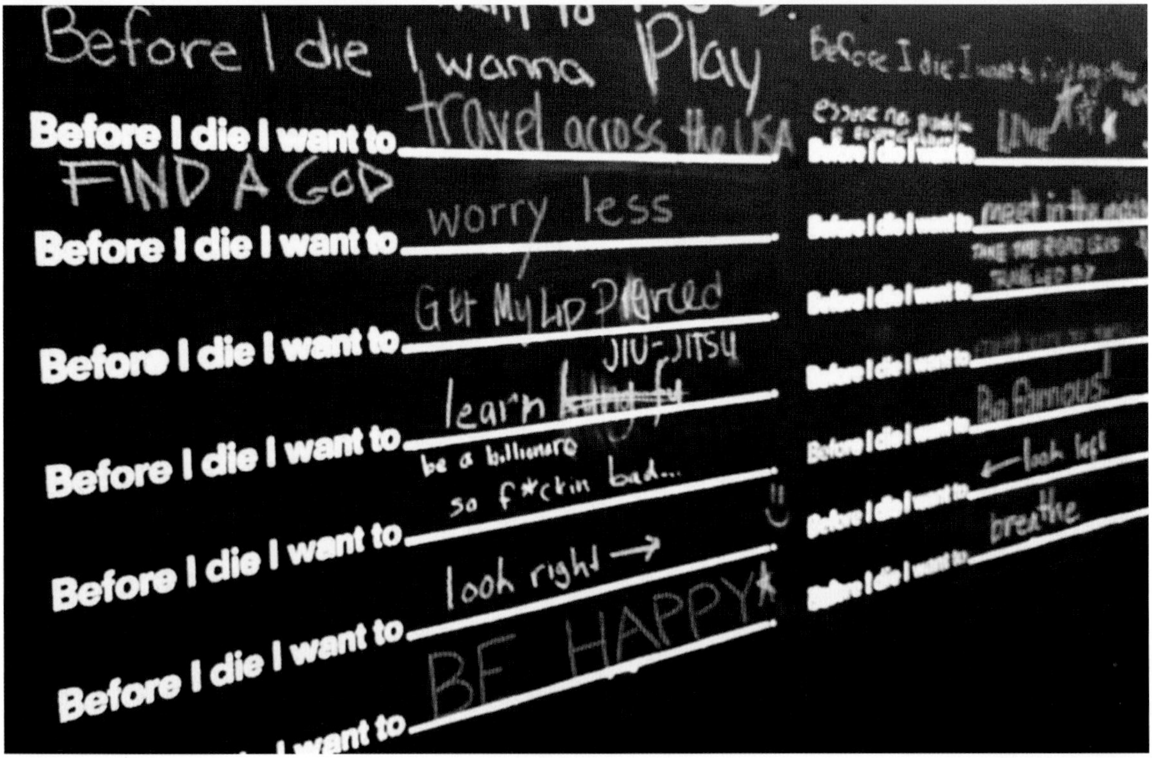

Cary Memorial Library

THE FIRST SHOT OF THE AMERICAN REVOLUTIONARY WAR WAS FIRED HERE
PAUL REVERE'S RIDE IS REENACTED EVERY YEAR ON PATRIOT DAY
POPULATION: 31,394

Lexington
Massachusetts

organized by
OLIVIA WENDEL & CARY MEMORIAL LIBRARY

Olivia Wendel was in high school when she had the moxie to organize a wall in her city. She partnered with her local library, which hosted the wall to a wide audience. "One man stayed for quite some time as we put the final touches on the wall," she recalled. "He was the first person to write on it and he smiled and wrote 'Read the complete Shakespeare's Works.' We applauded and he asked if he could write another. It was amazing to watch him take on this child-like glee. That's when I knew the project was accessible to everyone, surpassing age, gender, and disposition." Koren Stembridge, the library's director, said, "One of our students made the observation that the wall was like an analog Facebook update. It was interesting to see many of our older patrons — some of whom will never understand the appeal of social networking — becoming regular readers and writers on the wall." When the wall was dismantled, Koren kept a strip of it to hang in her office.

made with love by OLIVIA WENDEL, JAMIE YANG, DANIEL HARARI, TED ZHU, CECILIA YIU, MARLON ESPINO, IAN WENDEL, KOREN STEMBRIDGE, JENNIFER BUNTON FORGIT AND LIBRARY STAFF MEMBERS

OLIVIA AND DANA

Before I die I want to...

be as awesome as my daughter Olivia.

DANA'S STORY

My daughter Liv was 17 when she first saw a Before I Die wall and was completely dumbstruck by how amazing it was. She worked incredibly hard to get a public space and after many meetings, the town library agreed to let her curate the show in their lobby. She realized one of her dreams of helping her town and incorporating art and opening discussions. I am a very lucky and proud mommy.

Before I die I want to...

create more walls.

OLIVIA'S STORY

I was bored doing my homework one day and decided to take a break. Surfing the internet, I came across Candy's Before I Die project and was immediately drawn in. I knew that my town needed something like this — a reminder of the smaller, more essential lessons, rather than stressing over a bad letter on a report card. I didn't expect to get a response when I sent an email to the town, but I did from Cary Memorial Library. They were so helpful in putting it all together. Soon enough, we were painting on the stencils and it was dry, ready with a small bowl of chalk for people to write with. I could not wait to watch it fill up, a dream finally coming true.

I thought for a long time about what to write: *meet James Franco, eat the perfect veggie burger, have a recorded single released...* I've always been the kind of person who tries everything, so I had a lot of things swimming around in my mind. The first thing I wrote was "Before I die I want to experience the world." I've always wanted to travel. The next thing I wrote was "Before I die I want to create more walls," because the experience has taught me so much about my community and myself.

Cristina Zabalaga

HOME TO EUROPE'S LONGEST BRIDGE
BENEATH ITS STREETS LIES A HIDDEN ROMAN UNDERWORLD
POPULATION: 2.8 MILLION

Lisbon

Portugal

organized by
LX FACTORY

"Downtown Lisbon is an old city in ruins, metaphorically speaking, and we thought it could be interesting to use the walls of unoccupied buildings," said writer and artist Cristina Zabalaga, who helped organize this wall in the capital and largest city in Portugal. She and her friends installed a Before I Die wall on the side of an old warehouse in an area full of abandoned factories. The area sits just outside bustling downtown Lisbon, where there are many shops and restaurants. People pass by the old factories on their way to work or to the secondhand market that opens every Sunday. Cristina reflected, "One woman would stop to write something new on the wall every day. She would come very early in the morning because she didn't want anyone else to see what she had written. I thought it was lovely that she was so private about writing something so public."

made with love by CRISTINA ZABALAGA, PEDRO SOARES NEVES, RAMILSON NORONHA, INÊS GOMES, JULIANA ONO, AND MARTA FAUSTINO

Before I die...
Antes de morrer, eu quero SER UMA POMPADOURETTE!
Antes de morrer, eu quero VIVIR EN ESPAÑA
Ante er, eu quero CASAR CONTIGO ∞
eu quero SER UMA ESTRELA
u quero PODER DIZER QUE VIVI
quero iR a um concerto de Tracy Lee Summer!

Antes de morrer, eu quero FAZER UM SAFARI!
Antes de morrer, eu quero I'll laugh!
Antes de morrer, eu quero VIVER
Antes de morrer, eu quero tomar o pequeno-Almoço
Antes de morrer, eu quero tirar os óculos
Antes de morrer, eu quero APANHAR UMA BEBEDEIRA!
Antes de morrer, eu quero TER FILHOS
Antes de morrer, eu quero IR À LUA !!!
Antes de morrer, eu quero AMAR MINHA MULHER + 1 MILHÃO DE VEZES
Antes de morrer, eu quero
Antes de morrer, eu quero VIVER MAIS UM BOCADINHO
Antes de morrer, eu quero

Cristina Zabalaga

Before I die I want to...

repair my broken heart.

Before I die I want to...

play lots of pianos.

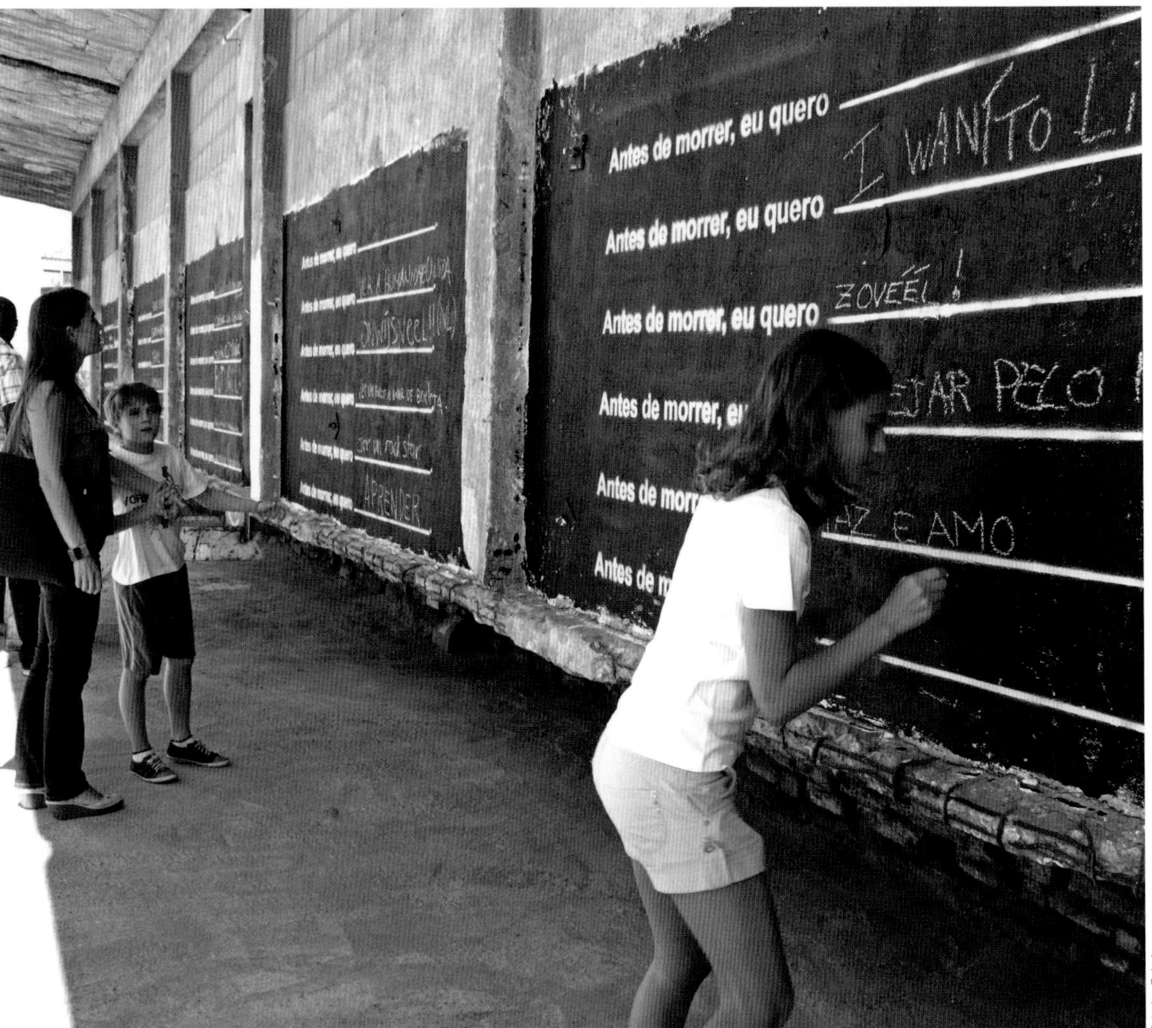

Cristina Zabalaga

Before I die I want to...

sleep with a harp player.

Before I die I want to...

visit the Taj Mahal.

Before I die I want to...

be the minister of education.

Alberto Vizcaino

PLAZA MAYOR WAS ONCE USED FOR BULLFIGHTS, TRIALS AND EXECUTIONS
PICASSO'S GUERNICA IS HOUSED IN THE MUSEO REINA SOFIA
POPULATION: 6 MILLION

Madrid

Spain

organized by
JOSÉ MÁRQUEZ

Near the La Linta metro station in Madrid lies a large and empty space. "There was a sports center here but it was demolished," said landscape architect José Márquez. In response, residents founded El Campo de Cebada, a project that encourages the temporary occupation of the vacant lot. José organized a Before I Die wall here, and replies included "spend a lifetime with you," "be able to express myself with music," "overcome the fear of living," "leave a story," and "see a just society," which echoed José's interest in using art to unify communities. "It felt like urban solidarity," he said. "People approached us, wondering what this was all about, and then they smiled. Some people wrote spontaneously and other people meditated on it for a long time. We hope this project will help us to recover the center that we lost."

made with love by JOSÉ MÁRQUEZ, DENISSE URDANETA, ALBERTO VIZCAÍNO, LAURA LARA, ANTONIO GARCÍA, MARÍA JOSÉ JIMÉNEZ, CLAUDIA MORA

Ingrid Langtry

KNOWN AS THE FOX CAPITAL OF THE WORLD
VEGEMITE WAS INVENTED HERE
POPULATION: 3.8 MILLION

Melbourne
Australia

organized by
LADRO GREVILLE

This wall is a permanent installation in Ladro Greville, a unique Italian bistro that raises bees on its roof for locally farmed honey. Their specialties include panna cotta with rooftop honey and Northern Italian pizza with goat cheese and honey. Their Before I Die wall is located in a secluded spot by the restrooms to give people private space to write on the wall without feeing embarrassed. "And since it's by the amenities," joked Ingrid Langtry, one of the bistro owners, "people will have had time to think about what they're going to write, if they've been sitting for a while." When the bistro hosts events, they rub the wall clean to invite everyone to write on it. "Then we'll take pictures and distribute them to the people who came to the event. It's a souvenir and a way of reminding people how fortunate they are to have what they do."

made with love by INGRID LANGTRY AND SEAN KIERCE

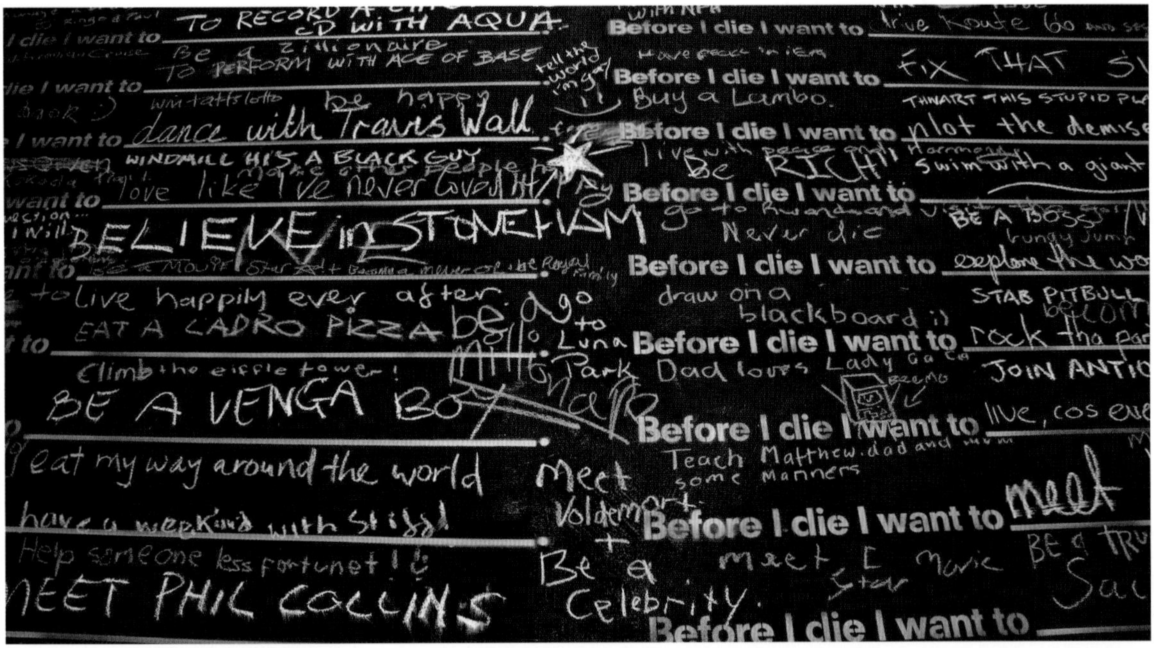

Ingrid Langtry

Before I die I want to...

surf seven days a week.

Before I die I want to...

fix that sink.

Before I die I want to...

wave to Earth from the moon.

Before I die I want to...

make my own birthday cake and eat it all by myself.

Before I die I want to...

drive Route 66.

Eduardo Krziminski

BISTRO OWNERS AND WALL CREATORS SEAN KIERCE AND INGRID LANGTRY

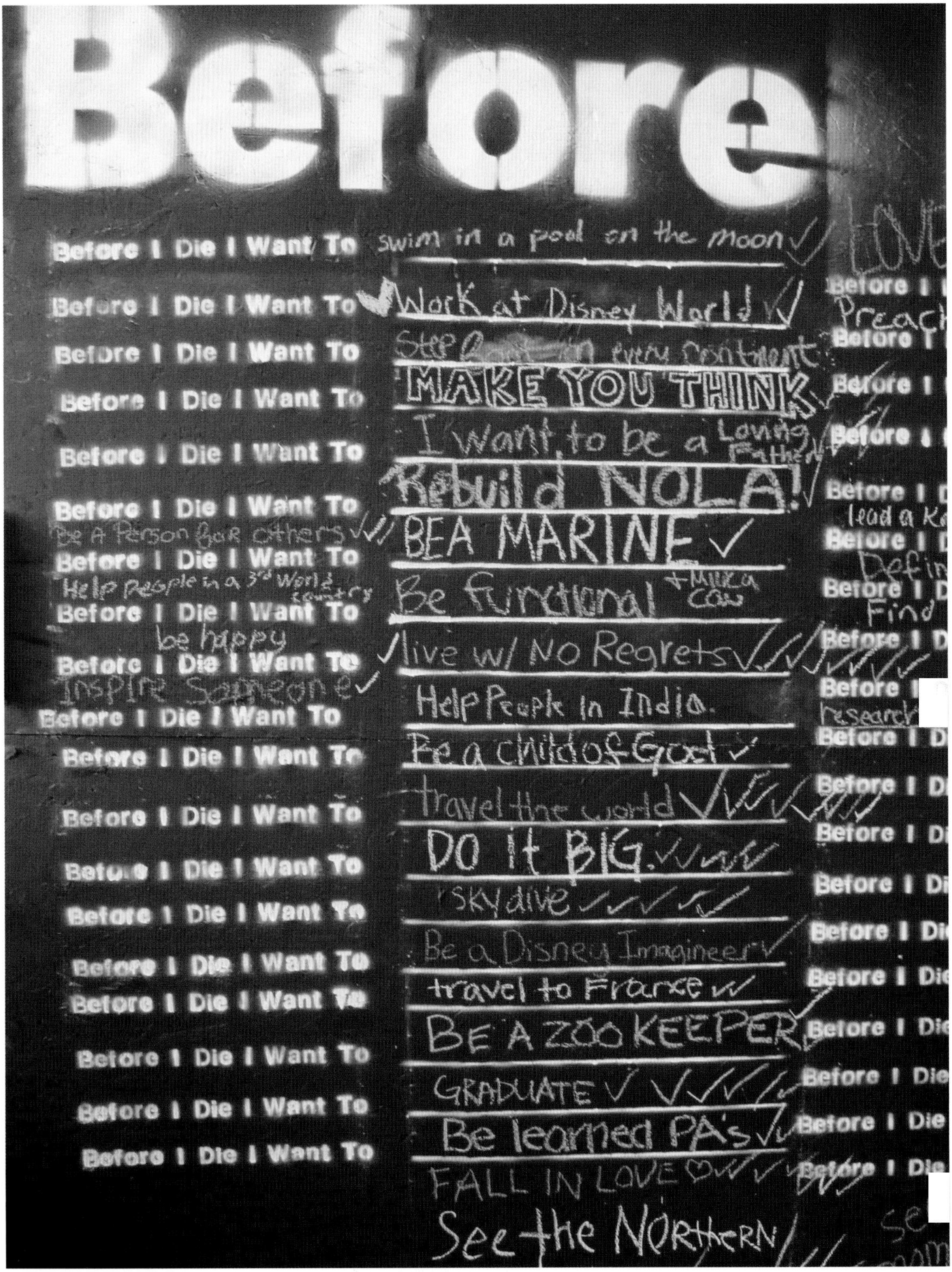

Alison Glaubke

NICKNAMED THE BEER CAPITAL OF THE WORLD
BIRTHPLACE OF THE TYPEWRITER
POPULATION: 597,867

Milwaukee
Wisconsin

organized by
MARDI GRAS MARQUETTE

This wall was installed by a Marquette University student organization after they found the original Before I Die wall online and drove to New Orleans to see it. "Afterwards, we knew we had to make our own," said organizer Charlotte O'Halloran, "so we made it in our basements and garages, and then we installed it under a bridge next to the library." The wall filled up immediately and led to interesting after-effects. Charlotte noted, "We were bummed because we didn't want to wash it, but there was no room left to write anymore, so people just started putting check marks next to the things they also wanted to do. It was cool to see the common bond between people. So often students have their heads down texting, and this allowed them to take a moment to stop and say 'what is that one thing I want to do?' It was also interesting to see another side of people, like the kid doing a keg stand last week who wrote 'I want to be a dad.'"

made with love by TOM NASS, MAGGIE BRUEGGEN, TOM KELLY, ALLISON GLAUBKE, MELISSA MAY, CHARLOTTE O'HALLORAN, ZACH BUCHHEIT, REBECCA HIXSON, HANNAH LADWIG, TYLER ATKINSON, ANNIE RICHMOND, AND PHIL LAROSA

Before I die I want to...

make someone's day.

Before I die I want to...

canoe the Mississippi.

Before I die I want to...

pass my Economy test.

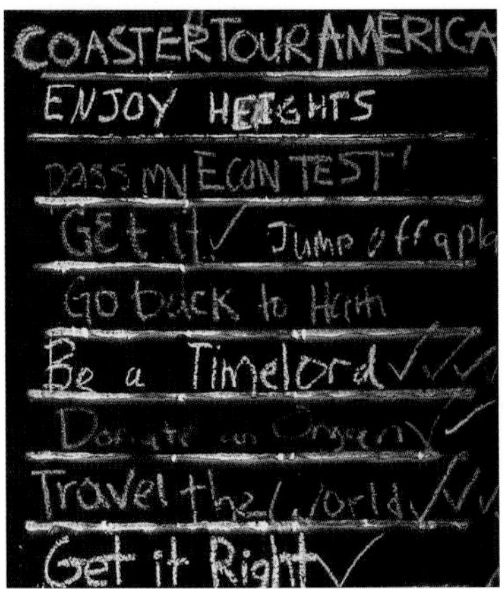

COASTER TOUR AMERICA
ENJOY HEIGHTS
pass my ECON TEST!
GET IT ✓
Go back to Heath
Be a Timelord
Travel the World
Get it Right ✓

Before I die I want to...

learn how to swim.

Alison Glaubke

Before I die I want to...

see my mom cancer-free.

efore I die
travel the WORLD!
Get dual-citizenship
Before I die I want to Peform at the MOMA
Sail With Gabi Around the world.
Tell Parent I'm Gay
Make Peace
go whale watching! become confide
Go Base Jumping
Become a Poke Mon Mast
Have 12 Boston Terriers
Have a gallery show
Before I die I want to have children.
live.
matter to so
Witness someo
SEE the GOSPEL
HAVE A FA
Have a family
truly Live
find love ← HELP YOU DO IT
BEAUTIFY MY 'HOOD!!
See my youngest Fly
Agape
See my future grandch
Make Ma
Zip Lin
SEE A SH
HANG A LI
SKY
MAKE ENOUGH
Walk my
The A
Fall i
ROAD
Before I die I want to
Candy Chang

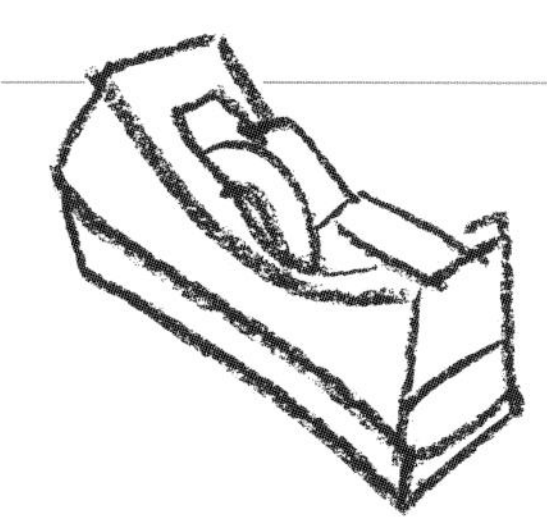

SCOTCH TAPE WAS INVENTED HERE
THE BIRTHPLACE OF PRINCE
POPULATION: 387,753

Minneapolis
Minnesota

organized by
ARTISTS IN STOREFRONTS

"We created this wall in a very do-it-yourself fashion, fronting the funds, and sourcing the public space to do it, then knocking the task out ourselves," said Joan Vorderbruggen, vivacious founder of Artists in Storefronts, an organization that transforms vacant storefronts into vibrant spaces throughout the Twin Cities. I happened to be in town when her wall was up and enjoyed meeting Joan and visiting the wall in person. A blank building facade between two beautiful murals became its happy home, where it collected many poetic answers, from "see my youngest fly" to "matter to someone." Joan's unbridled energy hasn't stopped. "I long to create a multilingual wall to reflect the over 100 languages spoken in this little pocket of Minneapolis!"

made with love by JOAN VORDERBRUGGEN, TOM SILER, SAM PITMON, AND SEORGE WURTZEL

Candy Chang

Before I die I want to...

tell my parents I'm gay.

Before I die I want to...

drive an ice cream truck.

Before I die I want to...

zipline in Costa Rica.

Before I die I want to...

fall madly in love.

Before I die I want to...

treat my husband the way he deserves.

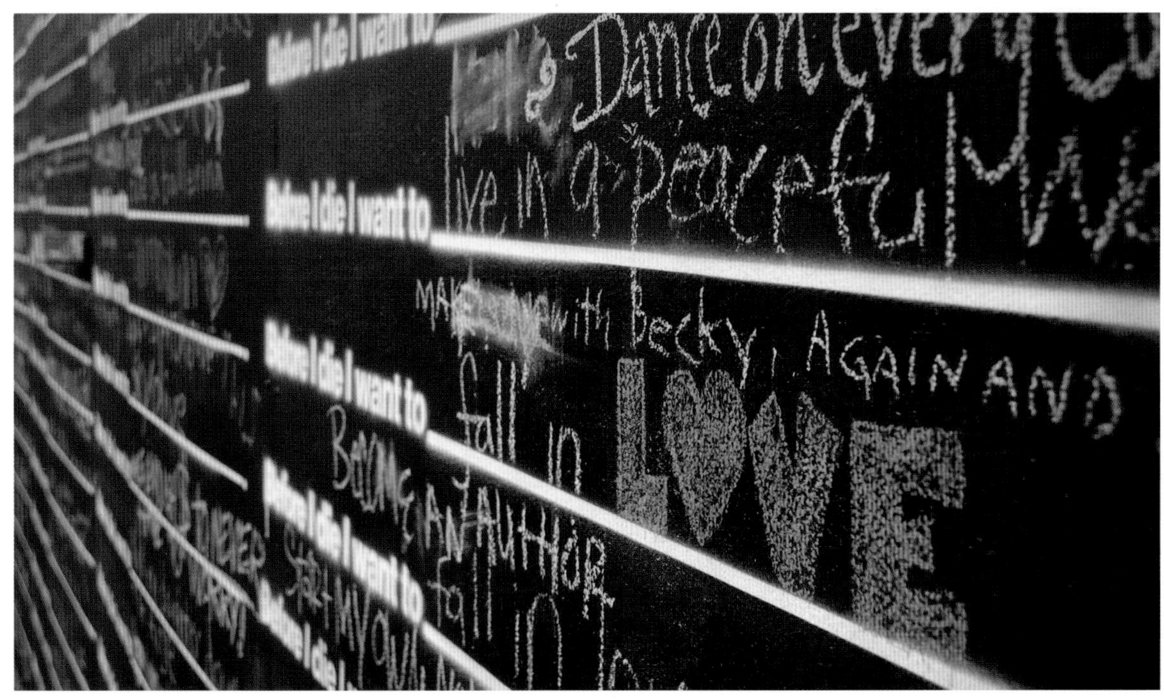

Before I die I want to...

move to Australia and become a citizen.

CHRISTINE'S STORY

I studied in Australia for six months before returning to the States and I cannot wait to go back. I feel more at home in Australia than I do in the USA. I'm moving back in 15 months — one month after I graduate. I save money every day: my barista tips, saving on my energy bill, refraining from eating out, and not buying things I don't absolutely need. I will return. And it will be the best thing I have ever done for myself and my happiness. Surf's up.

Candy Chang

Before I die I want to...

ride in a hot air balloon.

Sébastien Camden

HAS THE SECOND HIGHEST NUMBER OF RESTAURANTS PER CAPITA IN NORTH AMERICA
THE MONTREAL INTERNATIONAL JAZZ FESTIVAL IS THE WORLD'S LARGEST
POPULATION: 3.7 MILLION

Montreal
Canada

organized by
SÉBASTIEN CAMDEN & FRIENDS

Installed by students on the busiest street in Montreal, this Before I Die wall was the first to appear in French. "Universities in this part of Canada are required to teach in French to preserve our French culture," explained Sébastien Camden and Frédérique Brunet-Doré, who helped organize the installation in a neighborhood filled with people from all over the world. "In one day, we saw people write in eight different languages. One Sicilian guy approached us looking angry and demanded to know 'who did this?' We nervously told him that we did, and he yelled 'This is brilliant!' and bought us coffee. It was incredible to watch people stop for half an hour to chat or come back at the end of the day to see how everything was going. Some people wrote jokes while others wrote with their heart. One woman stared at the wall for almost an hour, then finally stepped forward and wrote 'I want to heal.' At that moment, we knew this wall meant something."

made with love by SÉBASTIEN CAMDEN, FRÉDÉRIQUE BRUNET-DORÉ, AND SAMUEL CHARLEBOIS-THIBODEAU

Sébastien Camden

Before I die I want to...

give away everything I own.

Before I die I want to...

heal.

Before I die I want to...

eat a good baguette.

Before I die I want to...

see you again.

161

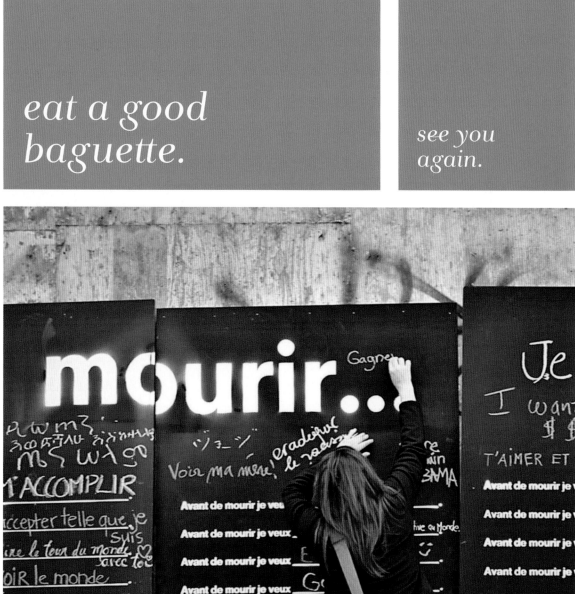

Before I die I want to...

meet an alien.

STEPHANIE'S STORY

Of all of the ways that the future could change in my lifetime, contact with a species not from earth would have to be the most profound. When I think of how foreign another human culture can be, and how fascinating the differences and similarities are, I am filled with wonder thinking about what there would be to learn from a culture from another planet.

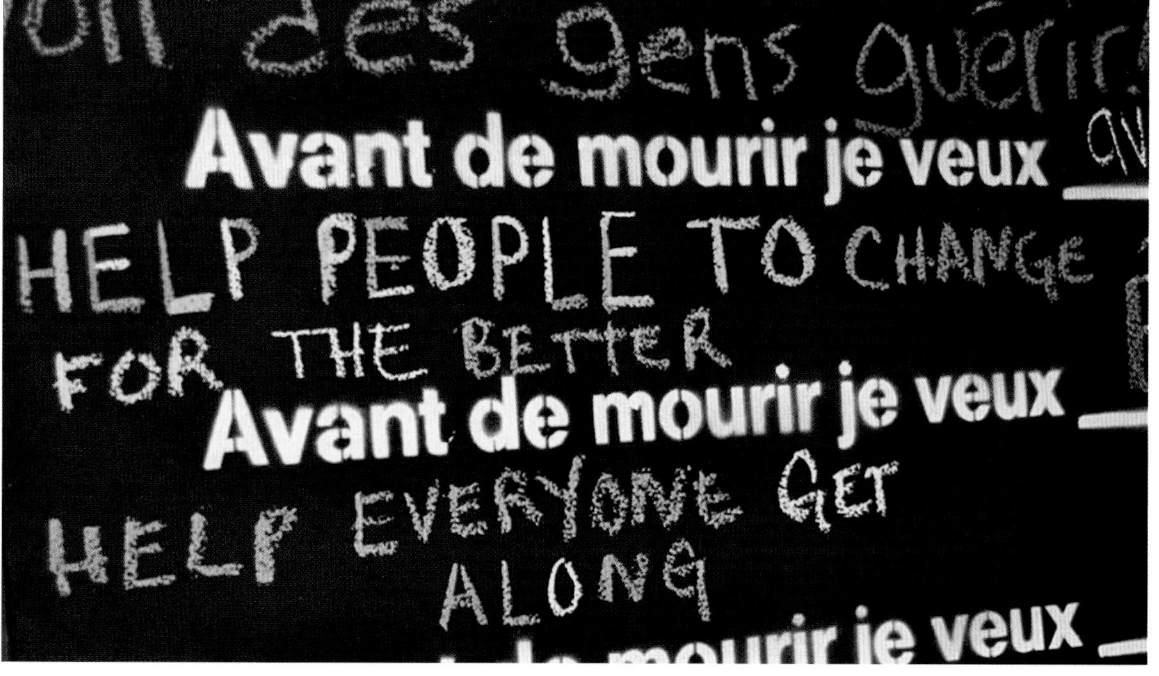

Sébastien Camden

Kristina Kassem

THE BIRTHPLACE OF ELLA FITZGERALD

NAMED AFTER CAPTAIN NEWPORT, WHO WAS SAID TO HAVE BROUGHT "GOOD NEWS" FROM THE SETTLEMENT

POPULATION: 179,611

Newport News *Virginia*

organized by
CHRISTOPHER NEWPORT UNIVERSITY

The pristine campus of Christopher Newport University got a little more colorful thanks to a class of students who built a great big portable plywood box as a communal canvas. A few hours before I gave a talk, we shook up our spray paint cans and stenciled while I asked them about their school. They were so sincere and close with one another, I could see the impact of a small class size, a passionate teacher, and a group of people who are ready to grow. The students wheeled the structure into Trible Plaza and it filled up with hopes that made me laugh and tear up. In the mashup were desires to "have an honest conversation with my mom," "fly a helicopter to Aruba," "find someone to love," "perform with a symphony," and "overcome depression." And sometimes hopes came together. Someone wrote "Before I die I want to meet a real man." Someone else wrote below, "Hi, I'm Alex."

made with love by MELISSA WILLIAMSON, RYAN GUNDERLACH, INHYE HONG, WHITNEY WALTON, KARIN DYER, MATTHEW RUTHERFORD, MICHELLE BRELAND, NICHOLAS DENSON, DIANE EDWARDS, SARAH WISTER, KRISTIN SKEES, ALAN SKEES, JILLIAN MARTIN, KRISTINA KASSEM, AND CANDY CHANG.

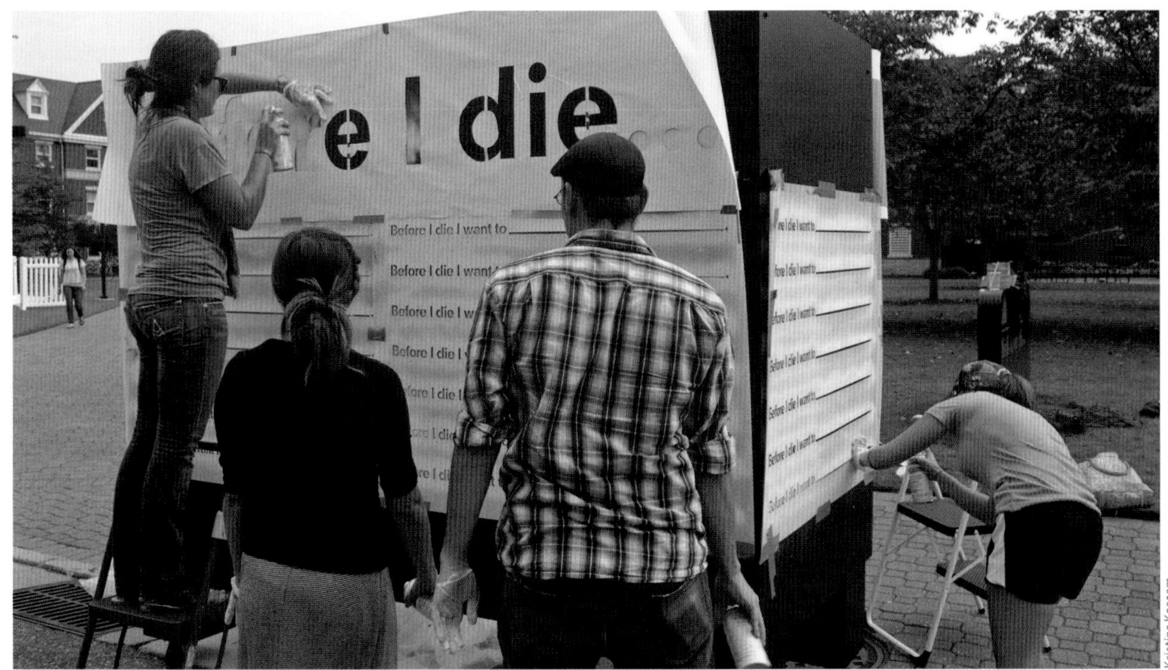

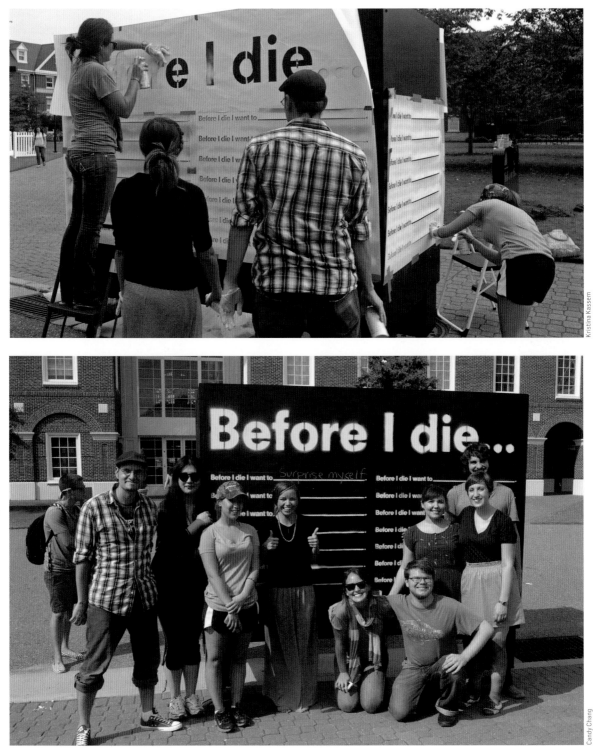

Kristina Kassem

Candy Chang

Before I die I want to...

see the amazing things my students will do.

KRISTIN'S STORY

My students and I worked together to install a Before I Die wall at Christopher Newport University to show how a single sentence, some spray paint, and some chalk can change the way we see each other and our campus. That class became more than a class — it was like its own experimental petri dish of ideas, excitement, and collaboration. We were all invested in each other in a way that doesn't always happen in my other classes. We had been planning the Before I Die installation on campus for about six months, and I didn't know what I was going to write until that moment. I looked around at my students, who had waited so long for this experience and were so proud to be the ambassadors of the wall. I saw how inspired they were, and I wanted them to know how much they have inspired me."

Before I die I want to...

have an honest conversation with my mom.

Before I die I want to...

tell her I love her.

Before I die I want to...

go on a cooking tour of Tuscany.

Before I die I want to...

let my walls come down.

Kristina Kassem

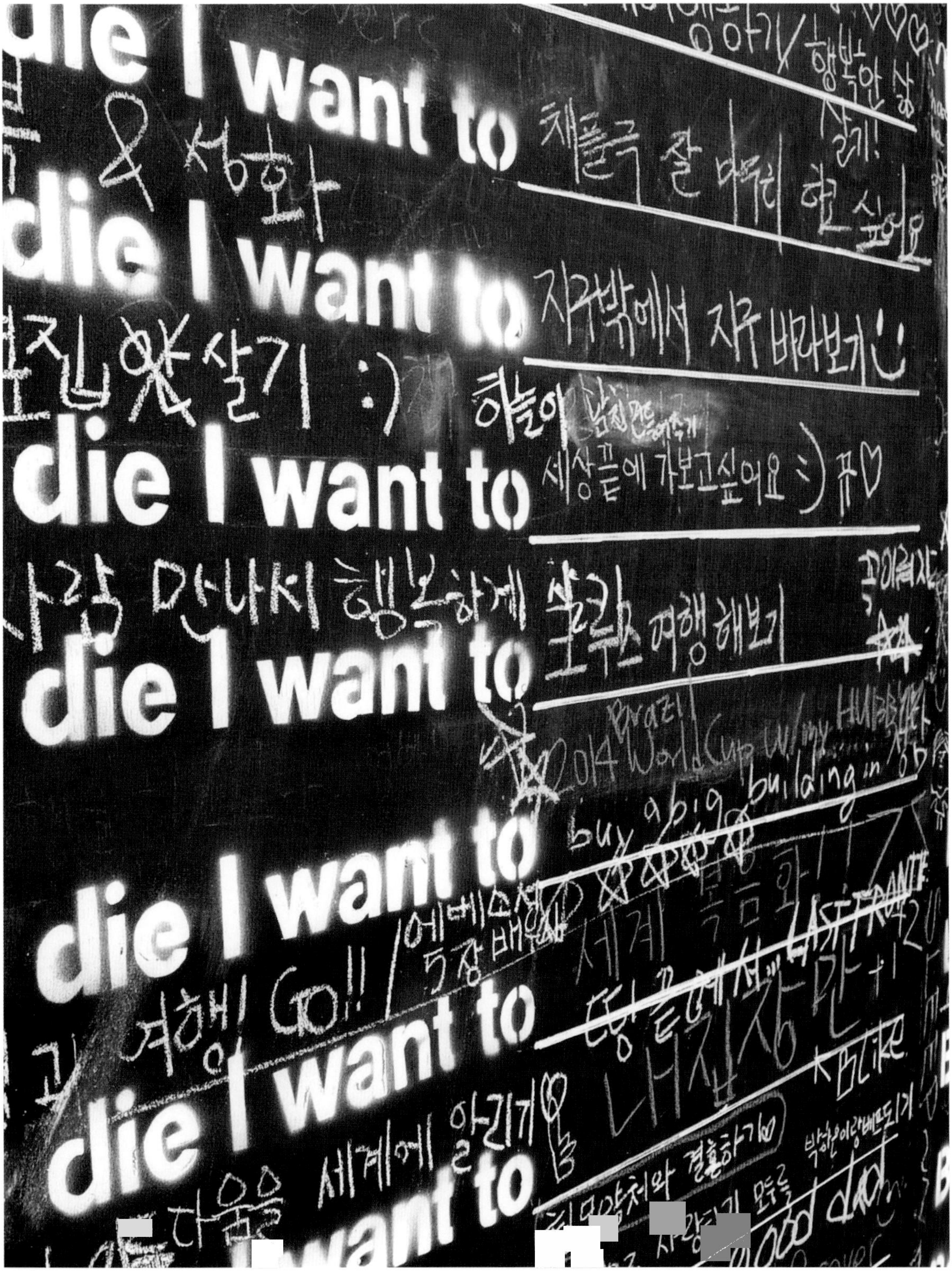

Shin Yuran

THE OFFICIAL BIRD IS THE SEAGULL
THOUSANDS GATHER AT THE ANNUAL SUNRISE FESTIVAL ON THE CITY'S BEACHES
POPULATION: 509,279

Pohang City
South Korea

organized by
HANDONG GLOBAL UNIVERSITY

As part of a school project, students at Handong Global University created a wall that included hopes from "hang out with North Korean children" to "stare at the stars with the people I love." The wall wasn't without drama. "One day strong winds knocked the wall down," said student Heo Yeonsoo. "After hearing the news I hurried out to the wall, only to find that someone had already fixed it. I was really touched that other people valued the wall as much as I did." The wall was up for one week and taken care of by the community, but its effects on Yeonsoo lasted longer. "Even though our tough, competitive society teaches us to see ourselves as rivals, we are the ones who can share the joy and make it double and share the sorrow and make it half-sorrow. We just need to look around and take care of our neighbors."

made with love by JUNG JINYEONG, HEO YEONSOO, LEE CHAEYEONG, JEONG DASOM, SHIN YURAN, KANG SANGWOOK, LEE ZION, HWANG JAEWOOK, CHAE JIYEA, AND JOSEPH LEE

Shin Yuran

Before I die I want to...

stare at the stars with the people I love.

Before I die I want to...

leave the army safely.

Before I die I want to...

introduce the beauty of a united Korea to the world.

Before I die I want to...

play soccer with my kids.

Before I die I want to...

build the most creative house.

Kristina Kassem

3S Artspace

WAS THE SITE OF THE 1905 TREATY ENDING THE RUSSO-JAPANESE WAR
WAS THE COLONIAL CAPITAL OF NEW HAMPSHIRE
POPULATION: 20,848

Portsmouth
New Hampshire

organized by
3S ARTSPACE

On the south side of Portsmouth lies Strawberry Banke, an open air historical museum and preserved 1630s New England village. When John Gale and Chris Greiner proposed to install a wall here, members of the historical society didn't think it would fit into the village and the project was almost turned away. "But the museum director defended us," said John. "He argued that the historical village was created to preserve the history and voices of people living over 300 years ago, and this contemporary installation does the same thing for people today." It was approved without further complaint and they created an impressive 32-foot-long double-sided, freestanding wall amidst restored colonial houses. "Our community really embraced the project and held it up as a successful example of how to present contemporary ideas in juxtaposition to history and tradition."

made with love by JOHN GALE, CHRIS GREINER, JANAKI LENNIE, BECKY LEROY, SHERYL CHATTERON, CELESTE LADD, GENEVIEVE GALLAWAY, EMMA MOREHOUSE, ALAN WILLIAMS, AND KRISTINA KASSEM

Before I die...
TRAVEL THE WORLD!
Make More Art
TWINS
Forgive him

SMOKE BLUNTS
LEAD A Revolution
Live life!
Before I die I want to
LIVE LIKE SCARFACE
give it All Away
SMILE
Save a life (or lives)
TRULY LIVE
Write a real Poem.
TRUST IN God

3S Artspace

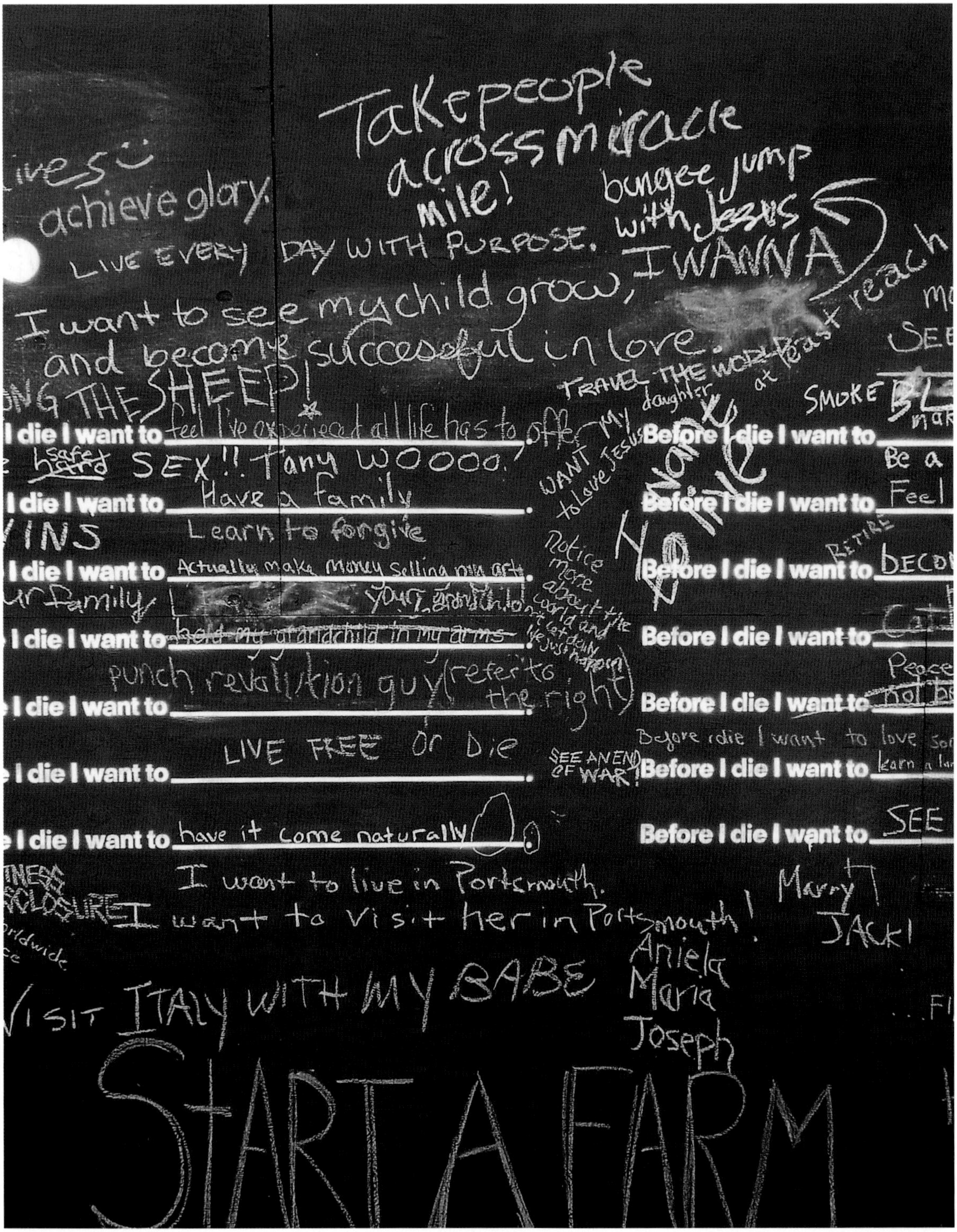
Take people across miracle mile!
achieve glory.
bungee jump with Jesus
LIVE EVERY DAY WITH PURPOSE.
I WANNA
I want to see my child grow, and become successful in love.
SHEEP!
TRAVEL THE WORLD
at least reach
SMOKE
Before I die I want to feel I've experienced all life has to offer
SEX!! Tany WOOOO.
WANT to Love JESUS
Before I die I want to Have a family
Learn to forgive
Notice more about the world and not let daily life just happen
Before I die I want to Actually make Money selling my art.
Before I die I want to hold my grandchild in my arms
punch revolution guy (refer to the right)
Before I die I want to
Peace
Before I die I want to love
LIVE FREE Or Die
SEE AN END OF WAR!
Before I die I want to
Before I die I want to have it come naturally
SEE
I want to live in Portsmouth.
I want to visit her in Portsmouth!
Marry JACK!
Aniela Maria Joseph
VISIT ITALY WITH MY BABE
START A FARM

3S Artspace

Before I die I want to...

live without a cluttered mind.

Before I die I want to...

be a mentor.

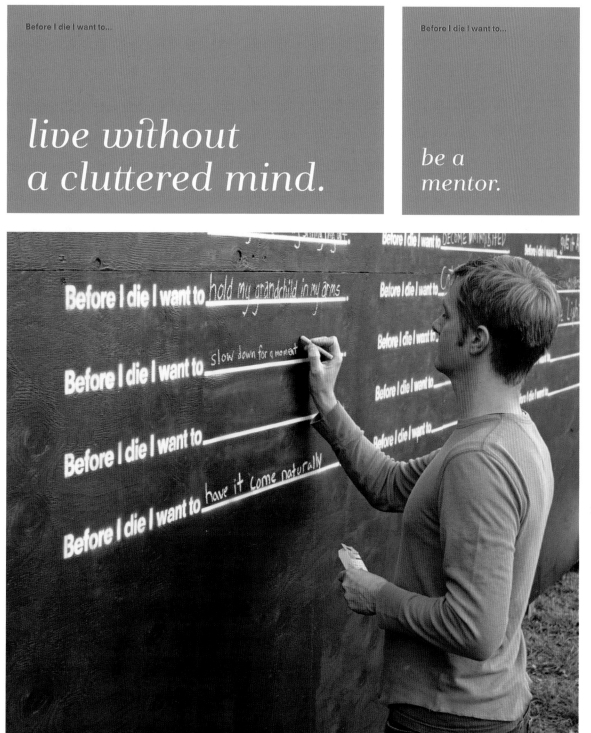

Before I die I want to...

really know my parents.

Before I die I want to...

see Portsmouth with a 24-hour food place.

Before I die I want to...

receive a carnation from the sad clown of life.

Before I die I want to...

sail across the Atlantic.

3S Artspace

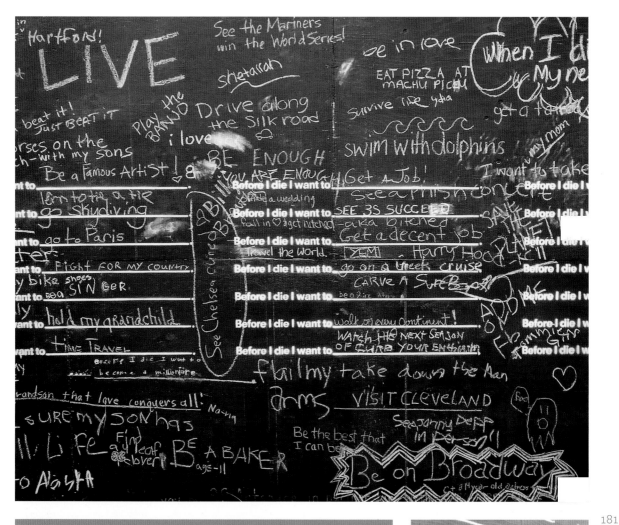

Before I die I want to...

slow down for a moment (and maybe even stop).

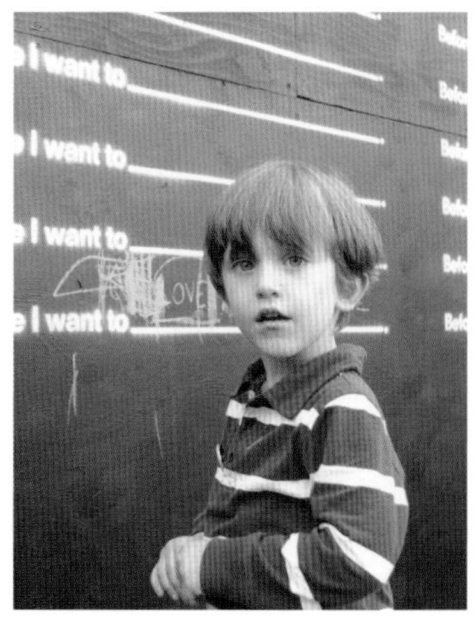

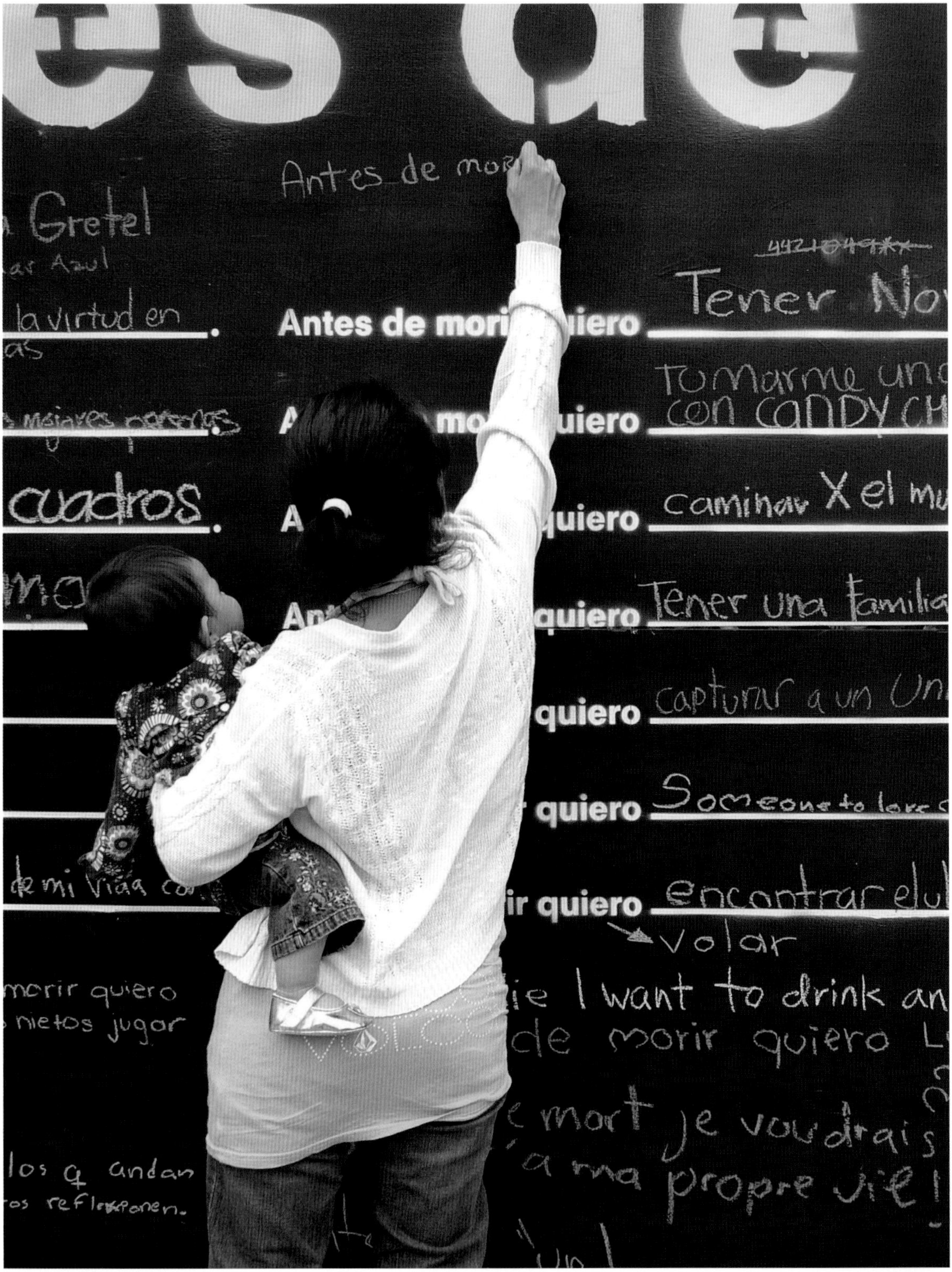
Antes de morir quiero
quiero
quiero
quiero
quiero
quiero
quiero
Antes de morir
Gretel
Tener Nov
Tomarme una
con CANDY CH
cuadros
caminar X el mu
Tener una familia
capturar a un Un
Someone to love
encontrar el
volar
morir quiero
nietos jugar
I want to drink an
de morir quiero
mort je voudrais
ma propre vie!
los q andan
Candy Chang

KNOWN FOR ITS BEAUTIFUL OPALS
THE MEXICAN CONSTITUTION WAS SIGNED HERE
POPULATION: 804 663

Querétaro
Mexico

organized by
CONGRESO FACTOR CLAVE

The taco never goes to the mouth. The mouth goes to the taco. I learned this street food-eating tip and wise new proverb in charming Querétaro, where conference goers and I created a wall in the busy Plaza de Armas. Twenty of us took turns stenciling a temporary construction barrier in the heart of the historic district, while construction workers, street vendors, and passersby looked on in wonder and confusion. After we finished stenciling it, we wrote our wishes and set the tone for others to join in. A constant flow of people came closer to the wall, read, laughed, and picked up a piece of chalk. Within hours, the wall looked like a new kind of Jackson Pollack painting. An old woman shared dreams of flying and a tiny boy wished to be a man and a husband.

made with love by ANA CECILIA SALAZAR SÁNCHEZ, OSCAR E. SALAZAR SÁNCHEZ, PAULINA LUNA PÉREZ, LUIS DANIEL REYES ORDUÑA, ANALUISA MONTES, SALVADOR HERNÁNDEZ CARBAJAL, OSMAR MORENO, EDUARDO MENA, TANIA DELAS CASA, ESTEFANIA MARTINEZ BRARO, MARIANA MUÑOZ MORENO, ALEJANDRA PÉREZ MÉNDEZ, SONIA PANTOJA NIEVES, ALEJANDRA MUÑOZ GARCÍA, REGINA MORÁN, TANIA ESPINOSA GÓMEZ, LAURA GABRIEL PÉREZ NAVA, MARIA JOSÉ BALBÁS LARA, MARÍA FERNANDA MELÉNDEZ GURIÉRREZ, JUAN ANDRES CACHO, KRISTINA KASSEM, AND CANDY CHANG

Candy Chang

friendly passersby

Before I die I want to...

travel to every continent.

Before I die I want to...

see a peaceful Mexico.

Candy Chang

Before I die I want to...

see the Aurora Borealis.

a las hermana
quiero ser esposo.

Candy Chang

Before I die I want to...

love someone more than my own life.

Before I die I want to...

tell the world I was very happy.

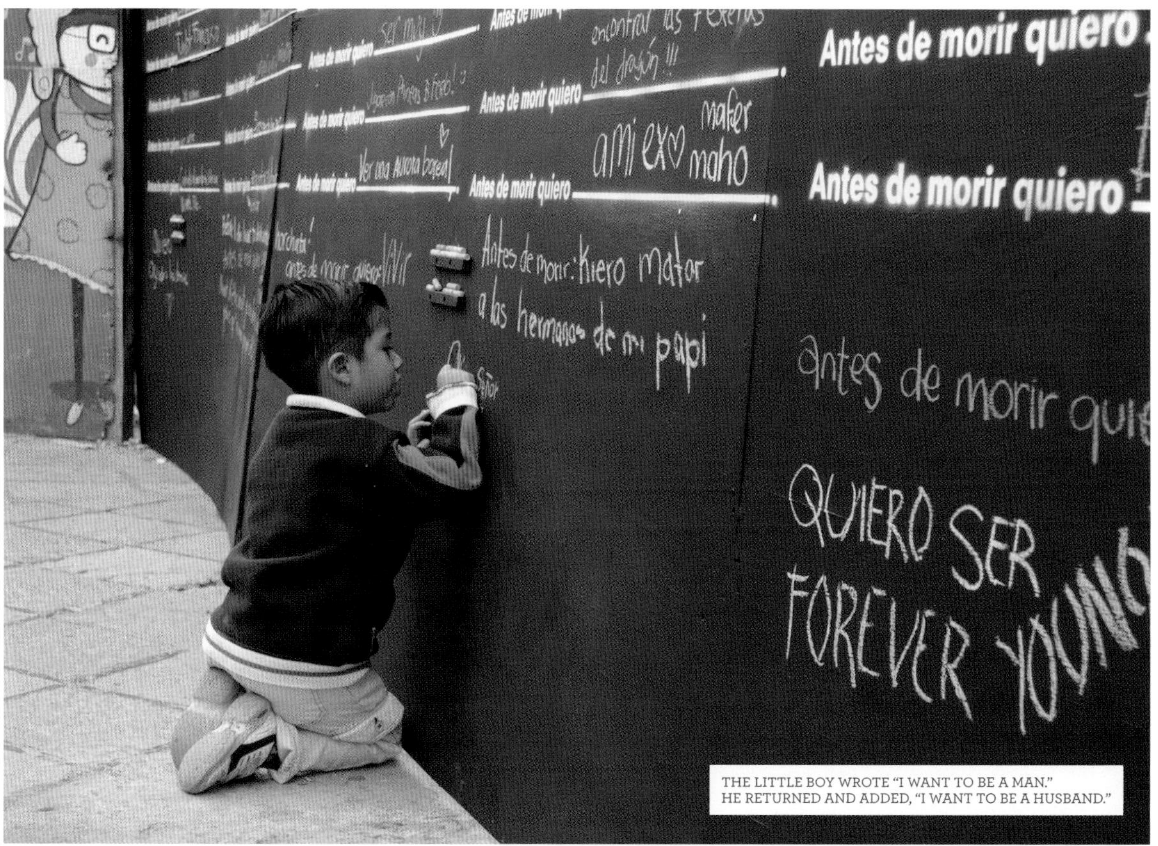

THE LITTLE BOY WROTE "I WANT TO BE A MAN."
HE RETURNED AND ADDED, "I WANT TO BE A HUSBAND."

Before I die I want to...

enjoy a deep kiss and a Havana cigar.

Antes d
Antes de morir quiero
Antes de morir quiero
Antes de morir quiero
Antes de morir quiero
Antes de morir quiero
Antes de morir quiero
Antes de morir quiero
Antes de morir quier
Antes de morir quier
Antes de morir quier
Antes de morir quier
Antes de morir quie
Antes de morir quie
Antes de morir quie
Before I die

Miriam Vargas

Kristina Kassem

HOLDS THE LARGEST FREE HOT AIR BALLOONING EVENT IN AMERICA
REFERRED TO AS THE DIVORCE CAPITAL OF THE WORLD
POPULATION: 227,511

Reno
Nevada

organized by
THE BLACK ROCK ARTS FOUNDATION

We painted and stenciled our hearts out under bold Nevada sky and billboards for gun shows. Thanks to the Black Rock Arts Foundation, the City of Reno, and the Nevada Museum of Art, I gave a talk and created two walls with local residents. One wall lived across the street from City Hall, which filled up with dreams to "bring my sculpture to Burning Man," "ski more peaks," and "attain financial independence." The other wall lived across the street from a homeless shelter and gathered desires to "stop drinking," "thank all the soldiers," and "find the bastard who steals my sleeping bags." Passersby helped us paint and entertained us with agile headstands on the sidewalk. One man wrote, "Before I die I want to see Mary again." I asked him what that was about. "Once upon a time there was a beautiful woman in my life. I messed things up. She left. I'm trying to become a better man so I can win her back. Life is better with love."

made with love by MARIA PARTRIDGE, SUSAN MOORE, BULL SCHULTZ, RICHARD JOHNSON, KRISTINA KASSEM, AND CANDY CHANG

Candy Chang

Before I die I want to...

support my parents as they supported me.

Before I die I want to...

bring more art into the world.

Before I die I want to...

live a clean and sober life.

Before I die I want to...

see gay marriage legal in all states.

Kristina Kassem

Before I die I want to...

be back in my kid's life.

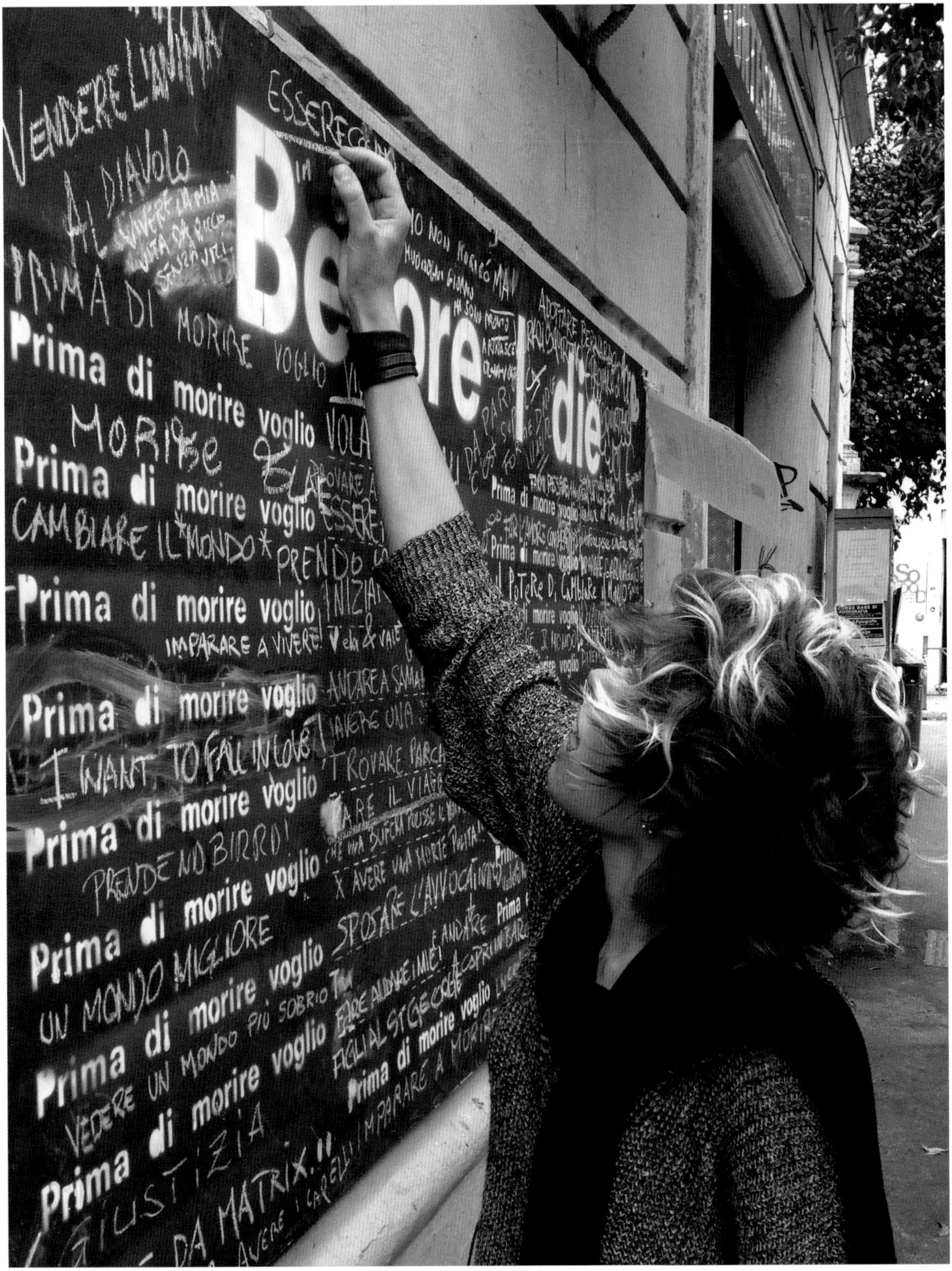

VENDERE L'ANIMA AL DIAVOLO
ESSERE
Prima di morire voglio
Prima di morire voglio
MORIRE
Prima di morire voglio
CAMBIARE IL MONDO
Prima di morire voglio
IMPARARE A VIVERE!
Prima di morire voglio
I WANT TO FALL IN LOVE
Prima di morire voglio
Prima di morire voglio
UN MONDO MIGLIORE
Prima di morire voglio
UN MONDO PIÙ SOBRIO
Prima di morire voglio
VEDERE UN MONDO
Prima di morire
GIUSTIZIA
DA MATRIX!!
die

G. Mazzaro

HAS A MUSEUM DEDICATED TO PASTA
HOME OF ST. PETER'S BASILICA, THE LARGEST CHURCH IN THE WORLD
POPULATION: 3.3 MILLION

Rome
Italy

organized by
CONTESTAROCKHAIR

ContestaRockHair operates ten hair salons around the world and their passion goes beyond hairstyling. "Our salons are also a showcase for art events and social awareness campaigns," said art director Alessandro Santopaolo. "Once we saw the Before I Die project, we knew it perfectly matched our world." They installed six boards in the company's first salon in the heart of an area of Rome called Pigneto, full of artists and musicians. "It was touching to see a Tunisian guy write that he wanted to return home to his wife," said Alessandro, reflecting on the response to the wall. "There was a cute elderly Austrian couple who wrote in Italian they want to visit Rome. And a drug addict, maybe in a hard clear-minded time, wrote that he wanted to stop. The boards filled up so fast we had to clean them every day to give everyone a chance to write. Soon we will spread the project in our salons worldwide."

made with love by ALESSANDRO SANTOPAOLO, COSIMO BARNABA, AND THE COMMUNICATION TEAM OF CONTESTAROCKHAIR

G. Mazzaro

Before I die I want to...

make my sons better people.

Before I die I want to...

bicycle all around Rome.

Before I die I want to...

have a socialist government.

Before I die I want to...

learn to be patient.

Before I die I want to...

find parking in this city.

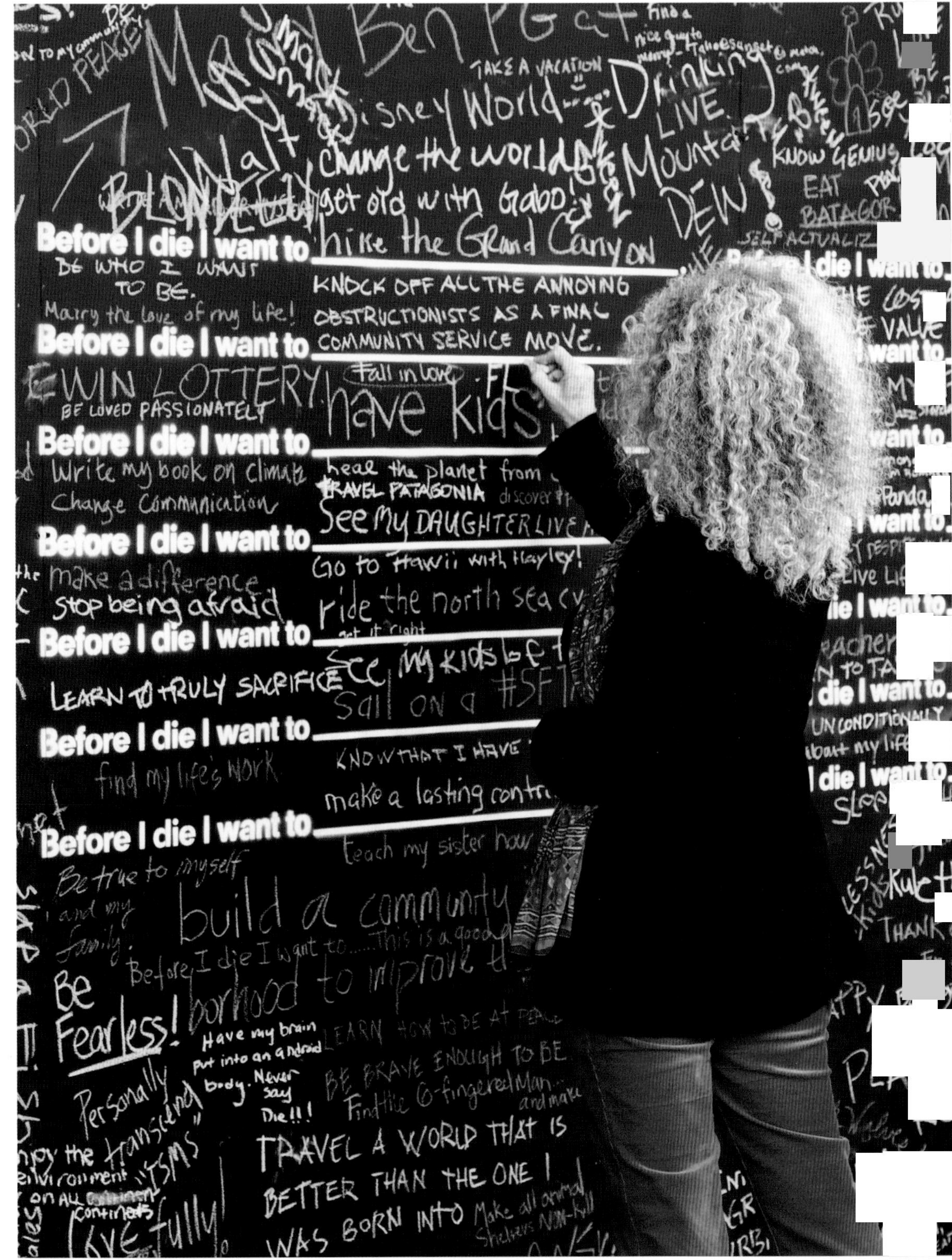

Before I die I want to.
Before I die I want to.

Kristina Kassem

THE BIRTHPLACE OF DENIM JEANS
HOME TO THE OLDEST CHINATOWN IN AMERICA
POPULATION: 812,826

San Francisco
California

organized by
GREENBUILD

In the heart of San Francisco's downtown district, Kristina and I stenciled a freestanding wall in front of the giant Moscone Center while boys offered free pedicab rides to passersby. As part of the Greenbuild International Conference and Expo, the wall soaked in a lot of green-minded hopes, from "write my book on climate change" to "witness our transition to full renewable energy." Other attendees and passersby shared more emotional goals, from "finalize my divorce" to "stop being afraid." A crowd came out after I gave a talk and within an hour the wall was crammed and colorful. I came back later to read the wall in solitude. The way people write is just as interesting and touching as what they write. "Inspire someone to be a leader" written the size of a gum wrapper added a humble touch. A tiny scrawl to "travel aimlessly with a backpack and my dog" looked so tender it made my heart melt.

made with love by THE GREENBUILD CONSTRUCTION TEAM, KRISTINA KASSEM, AND CANDY CHANG

Before I die I want to...

go fishing a million times.

Before I die I want to...

find what I'm looking for.

Candy Chang

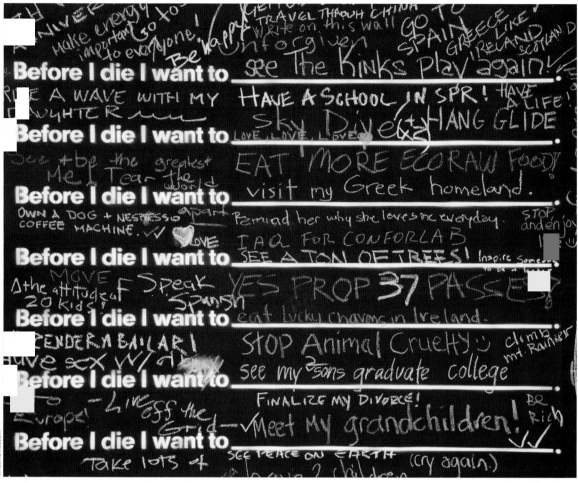

Kristina Kassem

Before I die I want to...

enjoy waking up early.

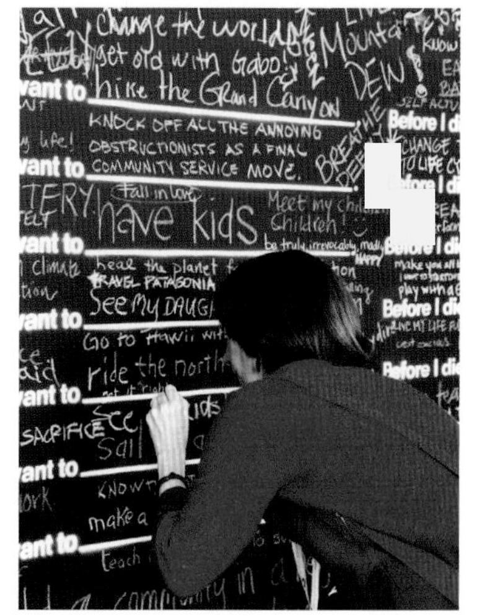

Before I die I want to...

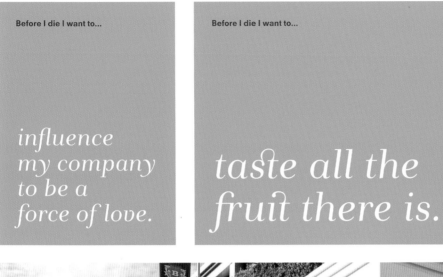

influence my company to be a force of love.

Before I die I want to...

taste all the fruit there is.

Kristina Kassem

Before I di
Before I die I want to
Become Batman!
Stop WAR
Improve my handwriting
Meet my sperm donor
Know God
Travel the world
Take a free pedicab ride!
Get published & travel through China
Go to Spain
Greece
Ireland
Be a mother
See the Kinks play again!
Have a school in SPR!
Hang glide
Build a true regenerative project
Eat more eco raw food
Get published
visit my Greek homeland.
Realize my dream
Meet my grandchildren
Fix us homeless
See a ton of trees!
Speak Spanish
Yes Prop 37 passes!
See the cure for cancer
Stop Animal Cruelty
see my 2 sons graduate college
Live forever
Finalize my divorce!
Meet my grandchildren!
aprender muchos idiomas!!
Lead!
Take lots of naps.
Retire
Write on this
End plastic pollution
Go to a Nick
Miss America

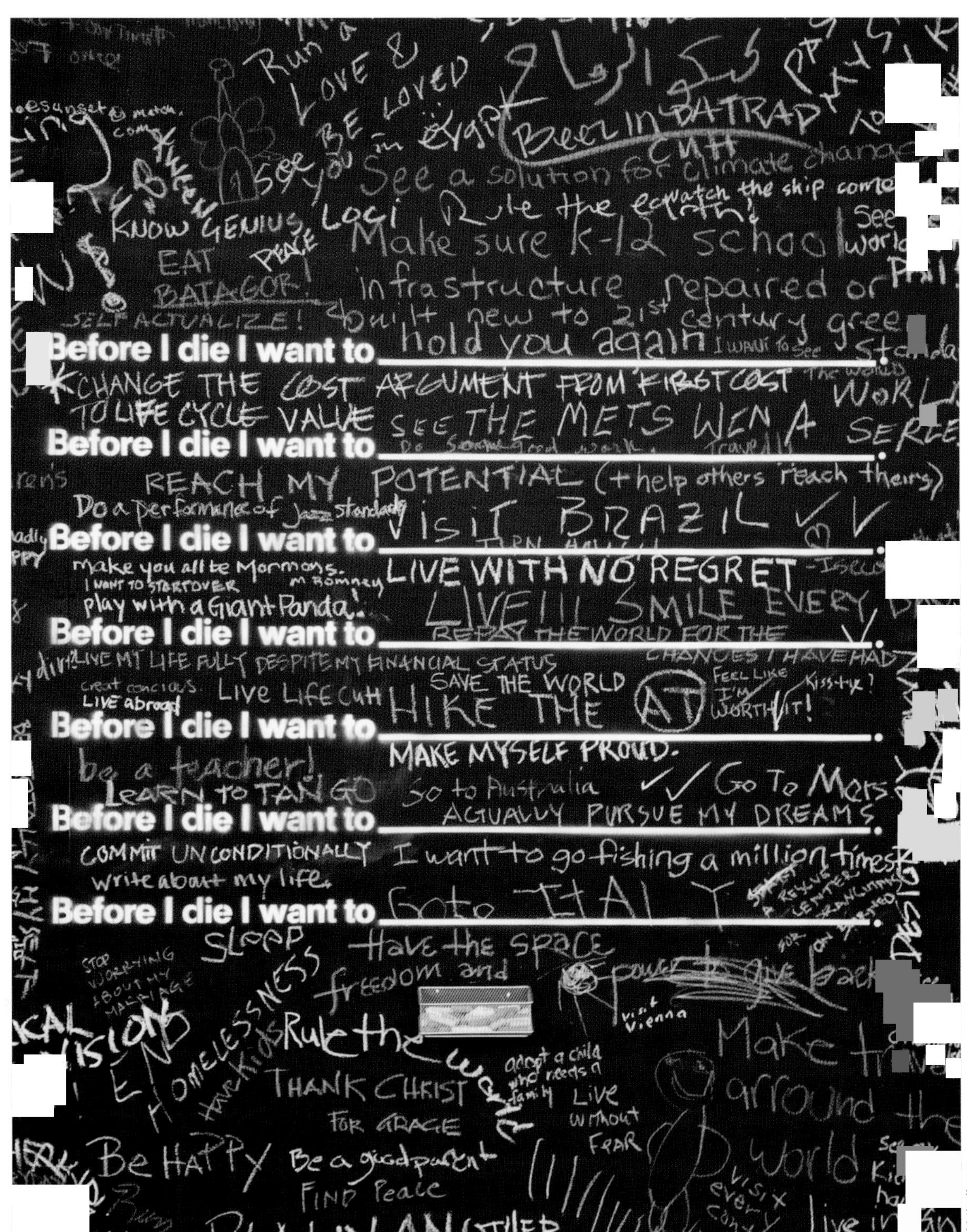

Kristina Kassem

Before I die I want to...

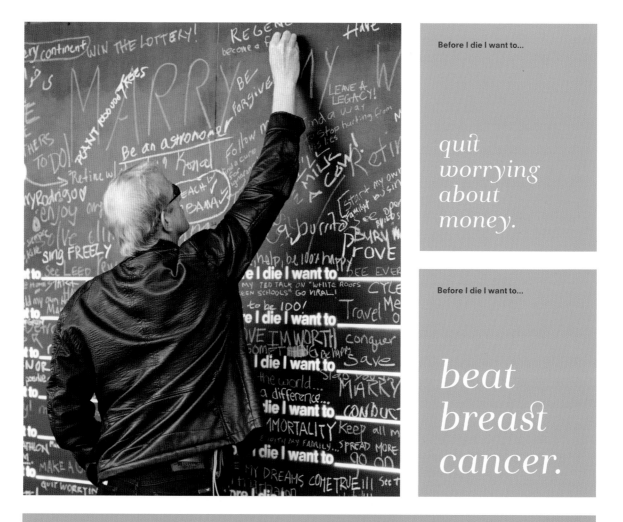

quit worrying about money.

Before I die I want to...

beat breast cancer.

Before I die I want to...

teach my sister how to surf.

SEBASTIAN BECA AND HIS DAUGHTER GABRIELA

Bernd Biedermann

WORLD'S LARGEST PRODUCER OF CARMENERE RED WINE
HOME OF THE LATE POET PABLO NERUDA
POPULATION: 5.8 MILLION

Santiago
Chile

organized by
SEBASTIAN BECA

When I heard Sebastian Beca's story I wanted to get on a plane and hug him. "I saw Candy's TED talk at breakfast one morning and said to myself, 'Before I die I want to build one of those.'" A week later, the computer engineer began hunting for unused walls and found an ideal location beside the Centro Cultural Gabriela Mistral, one of the core art and cultural centers of Santiago. His daughter was his main assistant and the wall was up for four months. "We estimate that over six thousand people wrote on it. We had to wash it almost every other day to make space for everyone." The wall had longer, touching repurcussions. "A couple of days ago my daughter was sharing one of her own creative ideas with someone who started doubting her. She said, 'You know, my dad wanted to build a wall and there it is.'"

made with love by GABRIELA BECA, SEBASTIAN BECA, LORENA TOLEDO, BERND BIEDERMANN, ÁLVARO BECA, CARLA FERNÁNDEZ, DENISSE VALLADARES, PAO SOLCITO, IGNACIO GIL, COTÉ CASTAÑEDA, POLI BECA, SOLANGE LECAROS

Before I die I want to...

be accepted by my parents.

feel that nothing was missing or left over.

Before I die I want to...

see Chile win the World Cup.

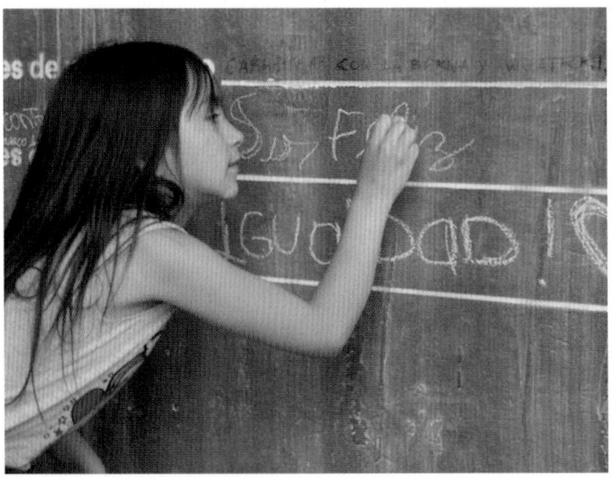

Before I die I want to...

have a talking dog.

Bernd Biedermann

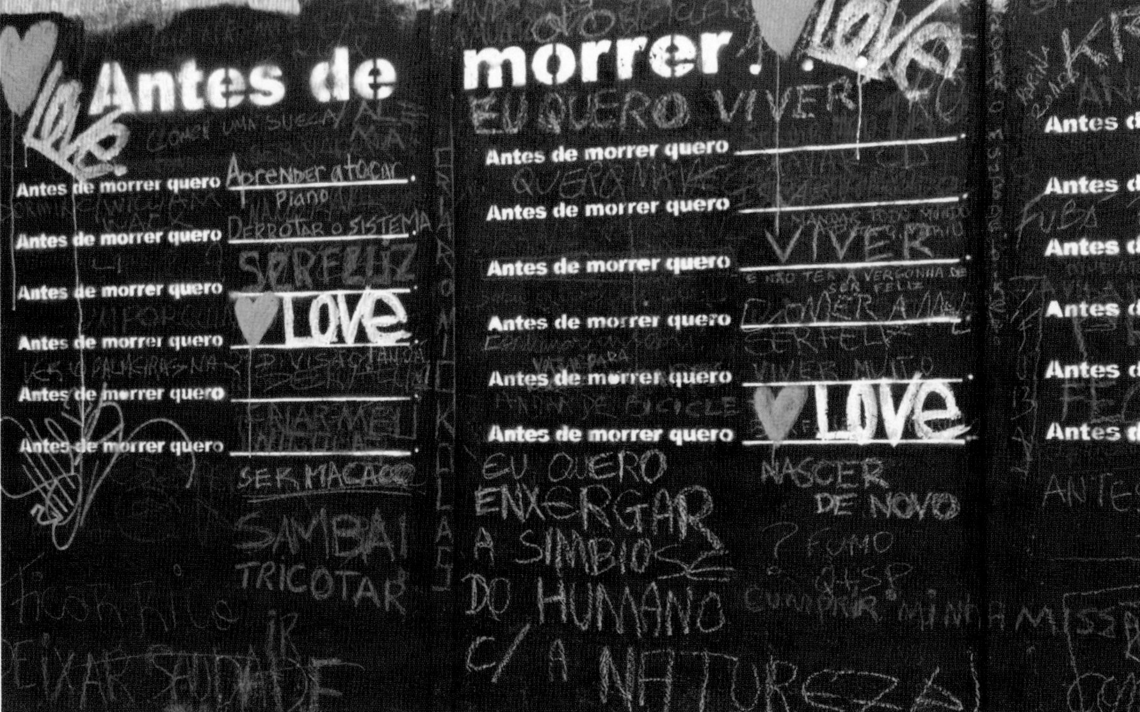

Laura Villela

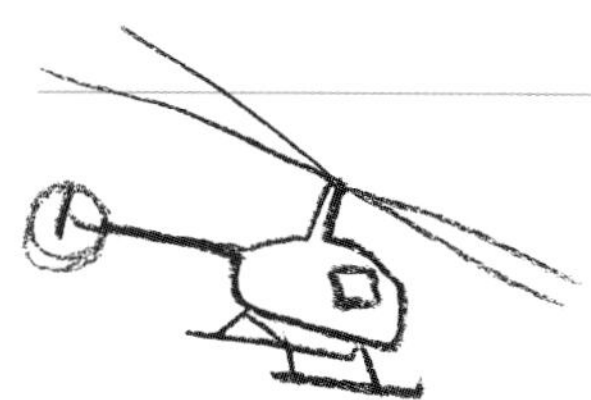

HAS THE LARGEST FLEET OF HELICOPTERS IN THE WORLD
THE LARGEST CITY IN THE SOUTHERN HEMISPHERE
POPULATION: 19.9 MILLION

Sao Paulo
Brazil

organized by
LAURA VILLELA & AARON PINCHEVSKI

After her grandmother passed away, Laura Villela decided to create a Before I Die wall near the cemetery where she was buried. "I made this wall in memory of her and created the wall as close to her as possible," said Laura. "She was an inspiration to me and she always told me that I should be happy in anything that I pursue. I wanted to pass this message on to others and have people reflect on what they want out of life." With help from Aaron Pinchevski, she created the wall on a construction barrier on Rua Cardeal Arcoverde, the same street as the cemetary. Responses included "swim in the sea," "take down the system," "walk on the moon," and "make it to age 18, because life isn't easy." "We weren't sure what to expect, but we were surprised to see so many people enthusiastic to share their dreams. This project has opened our eyes and made us realize that our time here is limited, and we should all spend more time doing what we love."

made with love by LAURA VILLELA AND AARON PINCHEVSKI

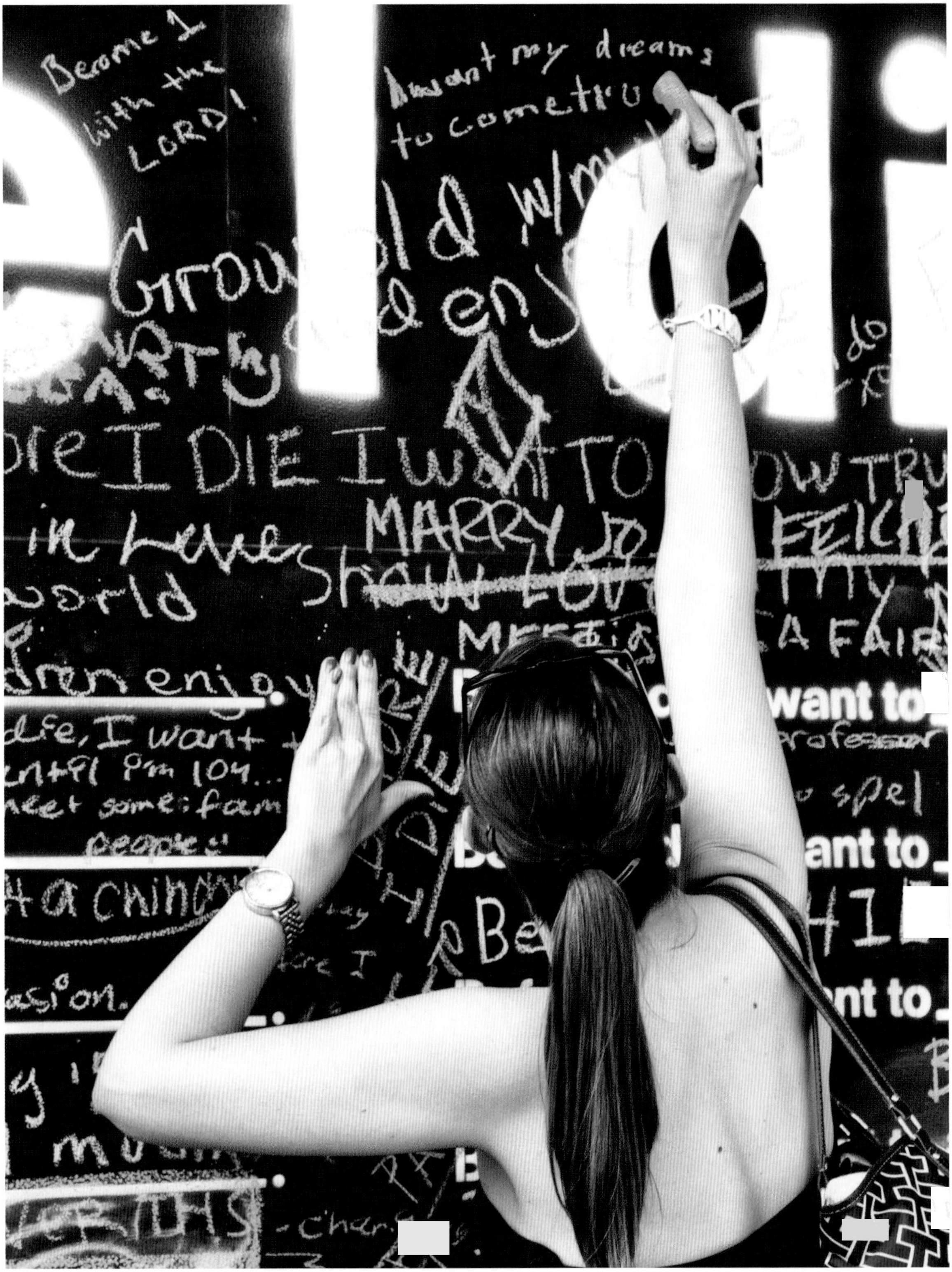

Trevor Coe

ONE OF THE MOST POPULAR WEDDING LOCATIONS IN AMERICA

DURING THE CIVIL WAR, A UNION GENERAL WAS SAID TO BE SO IMPRESSED BY ITS BEAUTY THAT HE COULD NOT DESTROY IT

POPULATION: 139,491

Savannah

Georgia

organized by
SEESAW

Savannah's historic district is one of the largest and most protected in the country. Organizers Megan Luther and Francis Allen created two walls — one in the Historic District on the side of an old bus station, and the other on Waters Avenue, a corridor of abandoned buildings and storefront churches with relatively high crime and unemployment. Responses such as "resurrect myself," "sing for an audience," and "be a hero" began filling up the incredibly vibrant walls and, as is the risk with any project open to the public, a handful of crude remarks appeared as well. "This infuriated a church lady who purported to represent the neighborhood surrounding the Waters Avenue mural, pointing out that there were churches around and that churchgoers had to walk past this 'disgusting' affront to their neighborhood," said Francis. "Interestingly, many church members would actually stop by the wall and write or read responses on their way to and from church."

made with love by MEGAN LUTHER, FRANCIS ALLEN, JAMES ZDANIEWSKI, AND MATT HEBERMEHL

Before I die I want to...

be in a healthy relationship for the sake of my daughter.

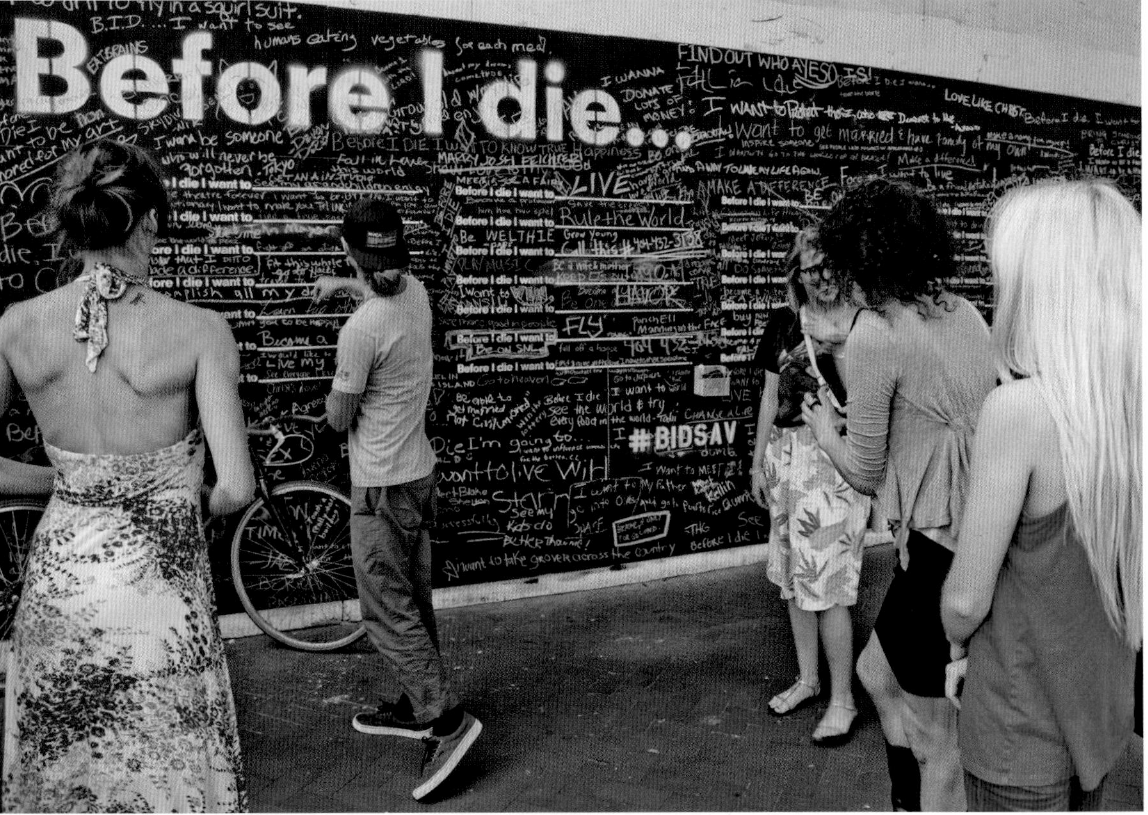

Trevor Coe

Before I die I want to...

overcome my fear of flying.

Before I die I want to...

climb a giant redwood.

Trevor Coe

Francis Allen

Before I die I want to...

quit smoking.

Francis Allen

Before I die I want to...

have a great love of my life.

Before I die I want to...

build a treehouse with my children.

James DrZ Zdaniewski

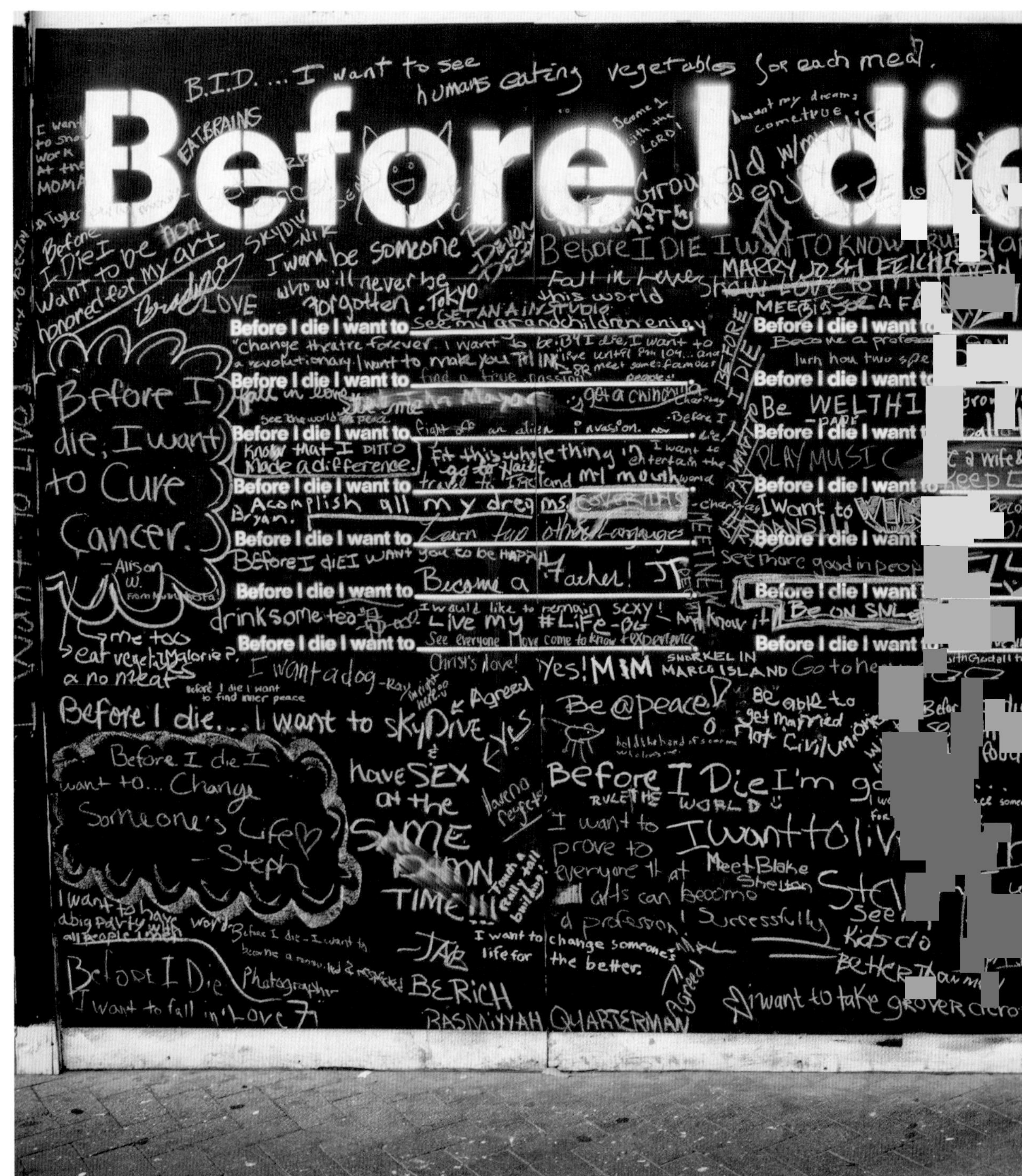
B.I.D. ... I want to see humans eating vegetables for each meal.
Before I die
Before I die I want to be honored for my art
I want be someone who will never be forgotten
Before I DIE I want TO KNOW
Before I die I want to
Before I die, I want to Cure Cancer. -Allison W.
Before I die I want to fight off an alien invasion.
know that I made a difference.
Acomplish all my dreams
Learn two other languages
Before I diEI want you to be HAPPY
Become a Father! JT
drink some tea
Live my #Life-BG
See everyone I love come to know
I want a dog -Ray
Christ's love!
Yes! M&M
Be @peace
Be able to get married
Before I die... I want to skyDive
Before I die I want to... Change Someone's Life -Steph
have SEX at the SAME DAMN TIME!!!
Before I Die I'm
I want to prove to everyone that arts can become a profession
I want to live
Meet Blake Shelton
I want to change someone's life for the better.
BE RiCH
Before I Die I want to fall in Love
BASMIYYAH QUARTERMAN
PLAY MUSIC
Be ON SNL
Be WELTHI
I want to take grover

LOVE. LIKE. CHRIST.
I WANT to Protect
Dearest to Me...
make a name
have family of my own
INSPIRE
I WANT TO GO TO THE
Make a difference!
FIND A WAY TO LIVE MY LIFE AGAIN.
I want to live
Be a friend
MAKE A DIFFERENCE
Before I die I want to
I want to drink
hug my boyfriend
make a
Before I die I want to
Before I die I want to
Before I die I want to
Before I die I want to
become a sister wife
BE A SWING PRO
Before I die I want to
buy new underware
Feel complete
Punch Eli Manning in the FACE
Before I die I want to
become A Model
FALL IN LOVE
Before I die I want to
TITANIC
DO Something
Before I die I want to
LIVE
CHANGE A Life
#BIDSAV
I want to MEET
BREATHE, IF ONLY FOR SECOND.

Trevor Coe

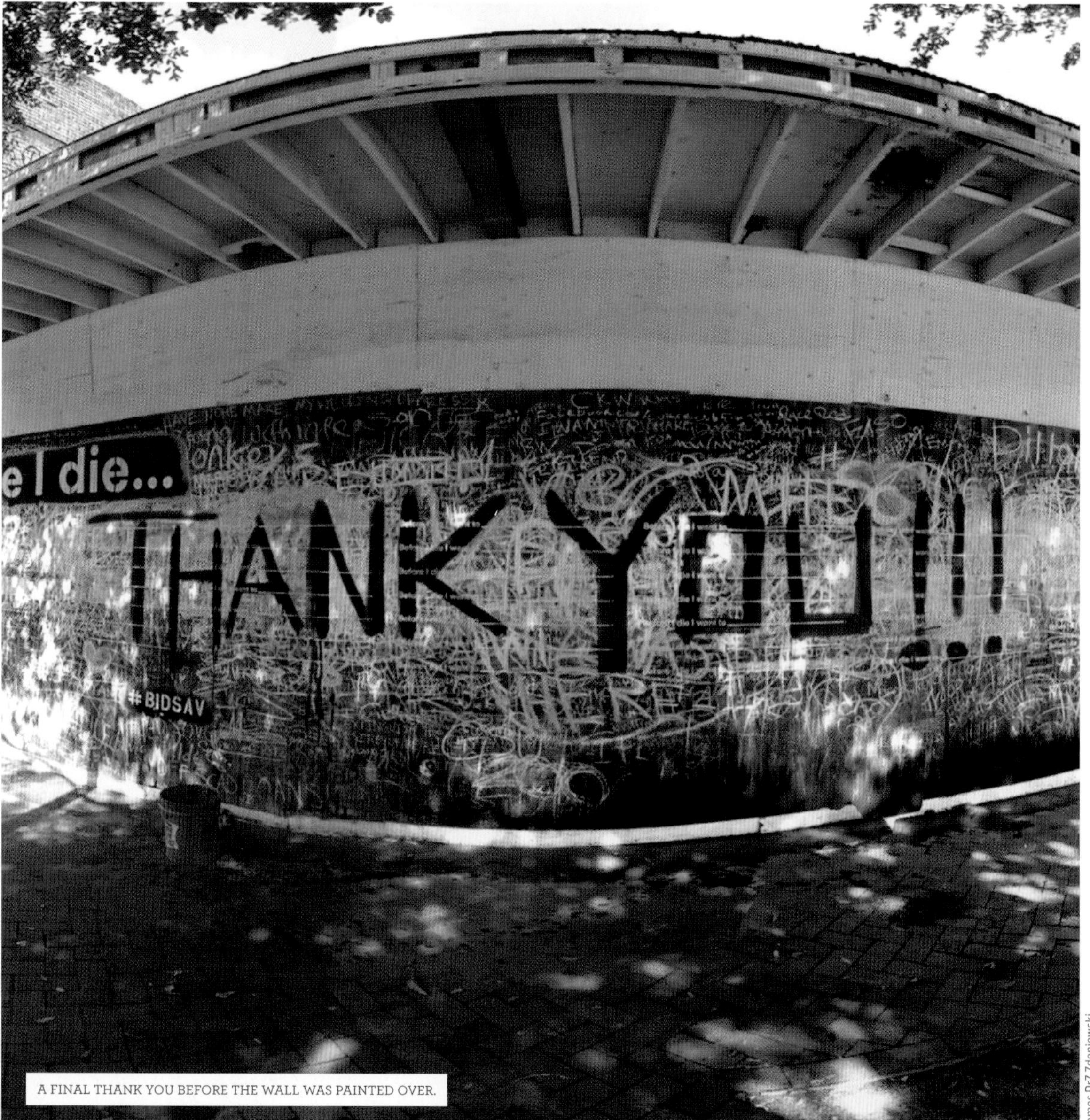

A FINAL THANK YOU BEFORE THE WALL WAS PAINTED OVER.

James DrZ Zdaniewski

Before I die I want to...

love like my dog.

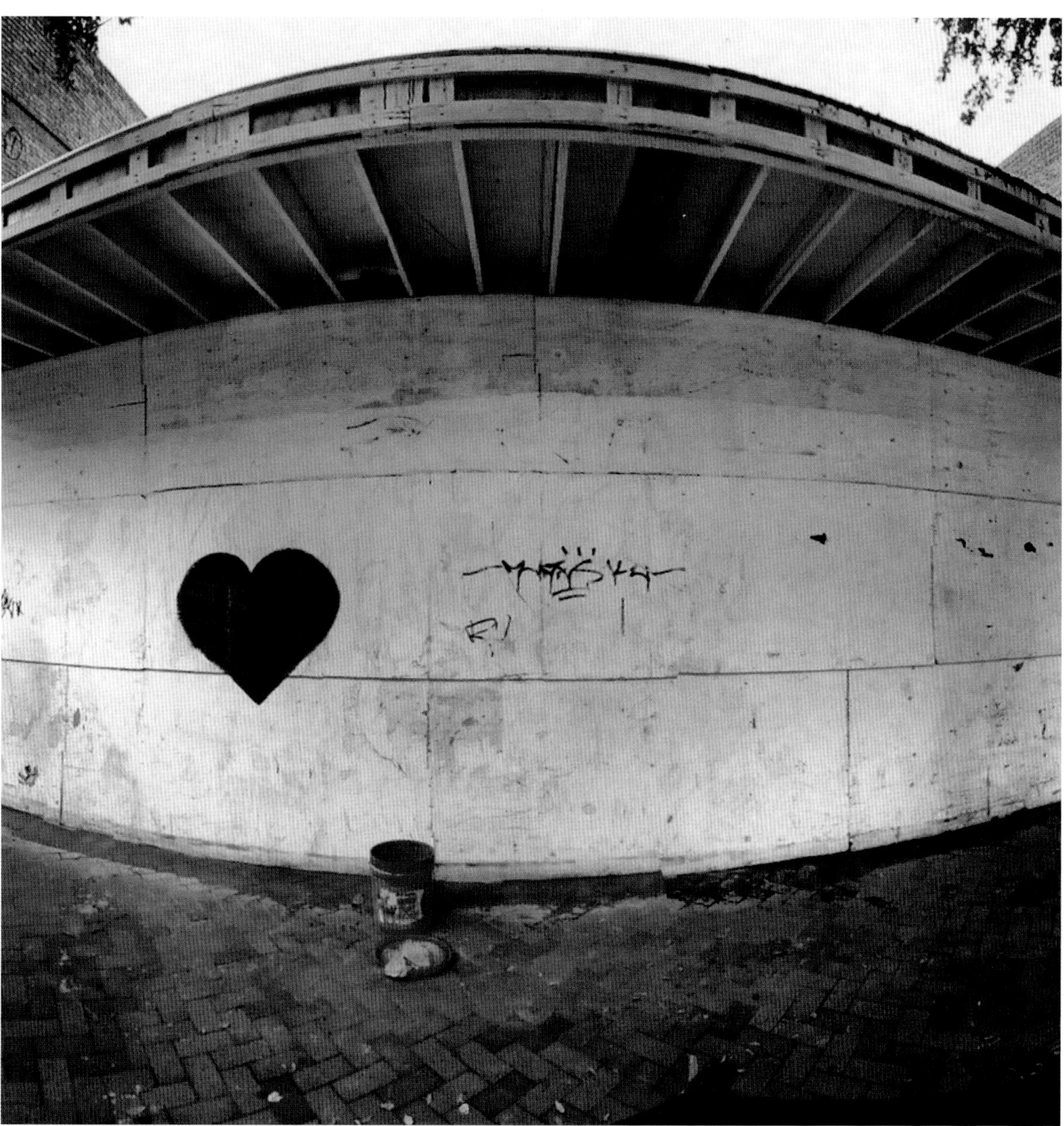

Before I die I want to...

give everything, fear nothing.

Before I die...
Before I die I want to ENJOY LIFE.
Before I die I want to LIVE!
Before I die I want to PAIN/CANCER FREE/LIVE PEACE
Before I die I want to See Earth from the Moon
Before I die I want to get rid of all regrets
Before I die I want to
Before I die I want to
I want to kiss the nose of a polar bear
travel the world!
TRY ANALYSIS
Save the planet!
Go Ballet
sky dive
Before I die I want to find

Kim Kamo

LARGE NETS ARE INSTALLED ON POPULAR BEACHES TO KEEP OUT STINGING JELLYFISH
DIVERS FLOCK TO ITS MAJESTIC CORAL REEFS
POPULATION: 180,389

Townsville
Australia

organized by
SMALL WORLD BIG DREAMS

When Kim's friend challenged her and a few friends to set up walls in different countries on the same day, she knew it would be a lot of work and that asking for help would be scary. "But I was excited to see what would happen, so I decided to just do it," she said. She created her wall from cardboard and at sunrise, she and a few new friends installed it in a waterfront park called The Strand. They spent the rest of the day on the beach observing people's responses. "Some would stop to read it," said Kim. "Others would rush up to it and immediately scribble something down. Then others would think about it for a long time before writing something." As for Kim, she thought about it for a long time before realizing, "What I really want to do before I die is to take care of my parents the way they took care of their parents in their old age, and the way they took care of me as a baby. I want to do the same thing for them."

made with love by KIM KAMO, JODIE RUMMER, JAY JACKSON, SUSANNAH LEAHY, AND MICHAEL KRAMER

Before I die...
LIVE LOVE LIFE
Enter WIPEOUT
See the Northern Lights
I want to
I want to
I want to
I want to
I want to
I want to
I want to
I want to
I want to
I want to

Kim Kamo

Before I die I want to...

swim with manatees.

Before I die I want to...

go to the stars.

Before I die I want to...

see where my grandma grew up.

Before I die I want to...

base jump off the Empire State building.

Kim Kamo

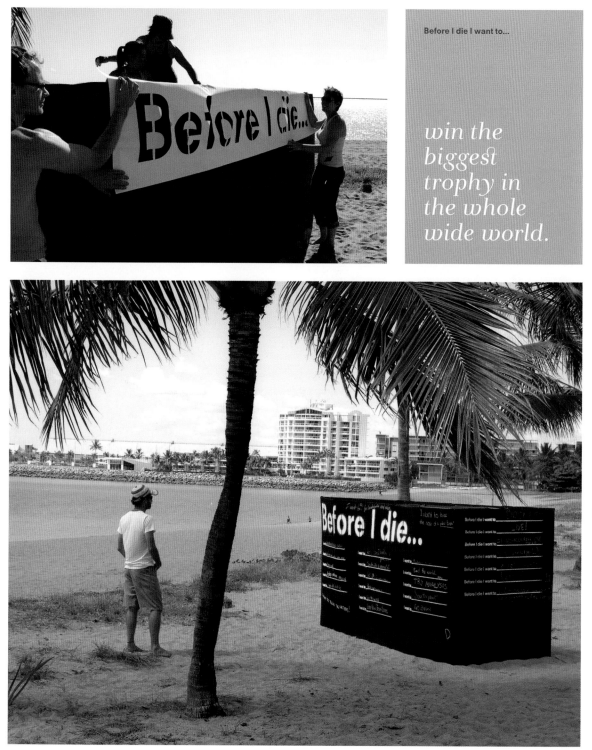

Before I die I want to...

win the biggest trophy in the whole wide world.

Antes de morir...
Antes de morir quiero
SER SUPER SAIAYIN!
¡Ser feliz!
Conocer todo el mundo
SER LA MANAGER DEL QUE QUIERE TOCAR
encontrarme.
vivir con Dios
saltar al vacío
Tener una hija con Silvana
TIRARME A MONICA SANCHEZ
QUE LA PLAZA DE ARMAS SEA MI JATO
tocar en un concierto!
Escribir mi vida en un verso
respirar, hablar y mirar con AMOR
volver a nacer
SER Vegana!
ser feliz

HOSTS A PERUVIAN PASO HORSE COMPETITION
THE WALL OF TRUJILLO WAS BUILT TO KEEP OUT PIRATES
POPULATION: 709,566

Trujillo
Peru

organized by
ARTES EN LAS CALLES

Founded in 1535, Trujillo is one of the oldest cities in Peru and known as the Capital of Culture because of its lively art scene. Arte en las Calles (Art in the Streets) is an artist-run organization that hosts monthly festivals in different parks around the city. "The theme that month was 'Dream On' so we felt the Before I Die project was perfect," said program manager Melissa Guadalupe Huertas. They found a brick wall in an empty lot and hired a construction worker to smooth out the surface with cement. Their wall collected hopes to "be a soccer star," "write a song about my life," "build a house for my mother," and "lose my fear of death" from grandparents, teenagers, and kids playing in the park. "Our goal is to create spaces where people can enjoy art for free while giving our local artists the opportunity to showcase their work. All of this in an evironment surrounded by the love and sharing of friends, artists, and neighbors."

made with love by MELISSA GUADALUPE HUERTAS, TULSI JULCA SALAZAR, JUAN LUJÁN, DIANA BENITES, AIDYN GONZAES, AND LEONEL RABINES

Elizabeth Sierra

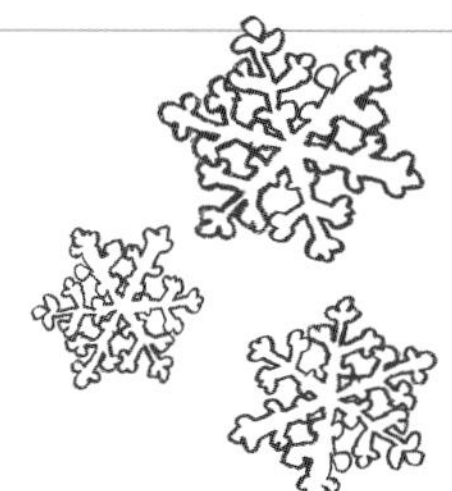

RECEIVES THIRTY FEET OF SNOW A YEAR
THE TOWN BEGAN AS A SCAM TO LURE PROSPECTORS OFF THE KLONDIKE TRAIL
POPULATION: 4,353

Valdez
Alaska

organized by
DR. ELIZABETH SIERRA & STUDENTS

Valdez is the snow capital of America, recently receiving a record-breaking 438 inches in one winter. "An outdoor installation was out of the question," said Dr. Elizabeth Sierra, who created this portable wall as part of her Death and Dying psychology course, a class I would like to take. She also plans to bring the wall to various events. Local hopes have included "write meaningful music," "meet my granddaughter," "live on my own in the woods," and "make a difference in many lives." "We were most interested in catching a glimpse into the collective psyche of our community by looking for common themes in people's responses," said Elizabeth. "This has been a wonderful way to get people thinking about the psychological and philosophical underpinnings of our hesitance to address issues related to life and living, death, and priorities."

made with love by DR. ELIZABETH SIERRA, CORI TAYLOR, ALEXANDER WILDE, PAUL TOPKOK, WITH SPECIAL THANKS TO WES LUNDBURG, CODY LEWIS, AND RYAN ADKINS

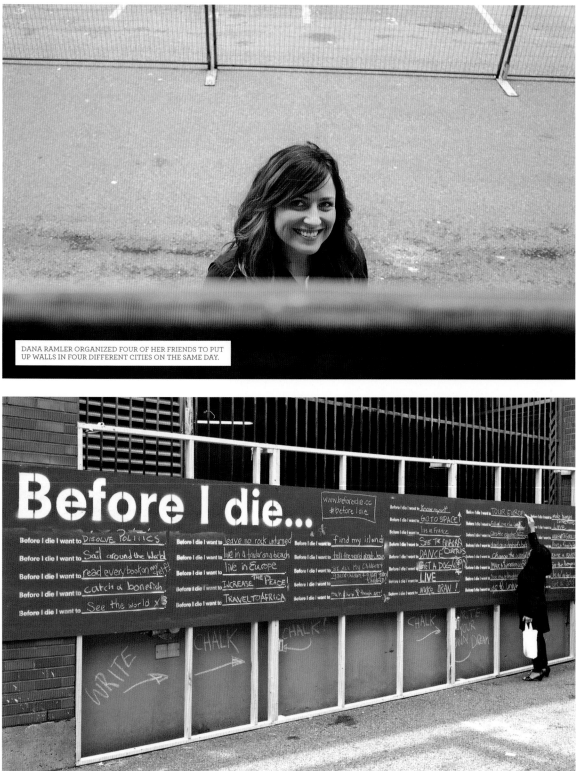

DANA RAMLER ORGANIZED FOUR OF HER FRIENDS TO PUT UP WALLS IN FOUR DIFFERENT CITIES ON THE SAME DAY.

Dana Ramler

NICKNAMED RAIN CITY
THE BIRTHPLACE OF THE CHINESE BUFFET
POPULATION: 603,502

Vancouver
Canada

organized by
SMALL WORLD BIG DREAMS

Dana Ramler is the mastermind who organized four of her friends to build walls on the same day in Berlin, Jersey City, and Townsville, Australia. She installed her wall on the side of a parking lot that faced an alley in a broken down part of Vancouver. "Because of the location, I was worried the wall would sit empty," said Dana, "But the alley ended up being a shortcut between two busy streets. And when a parade went through the neighborhood, the wall became a cool spot to hang out." The most touching story she heard came from an old man who wrote, "Before I die, I want to go back home." He explained that he left home at seventeen after being abused and had never returned. "He never realized he wanted to do this before he saw the board. But because it was anonymous, he felt like he could reveal his deepest desire. And because he had written it down — because he had declared it — he felt accountable to go and do it."

made with love by DANA RAMLER, BRYAN RITE, NATHAN RAMLER, AND ERIN EMMERSON

Before I die I want to...

ride a motorcycle to South America.

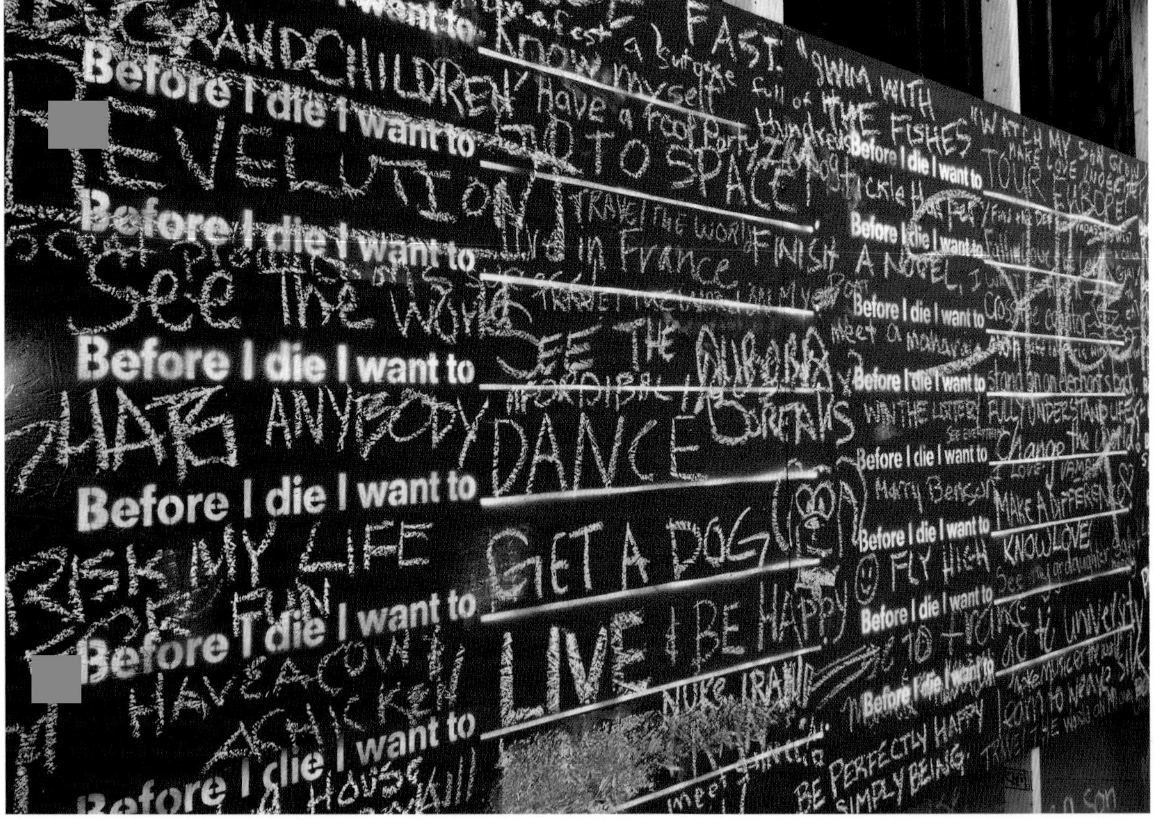

Dana Ramler

Before I die I want to...

read every book on my shelf.

Before I die I want to...

learn to weave silk in rural Japan.

Before I die I want to...

see a woman become president.

Before I die I want to...

leave no rock unturned.

Before I die I want to...

live in a trailer on the beach.

Forum Fermento / Cinema Teatro Primavera

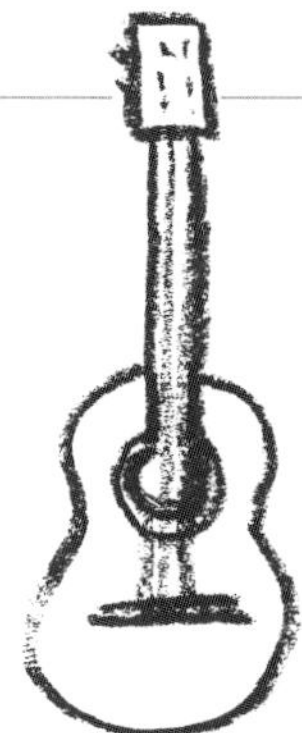

HOSTS AN ANNUAL GUITAR FESTIVAL
THE ITALIAN CAPITAL OF GOLDSMITHERY
POPULATION: 115,927

Vicenza
Italy

organized by
FORUM FERMENTO / CINEMA TEATRO PRIMAVERA

Sean Michael Hall describes Vicenza as "one of the most beautiful places in Italy, home to all the famous villas designed by Palladio." It is also home to a neglected 1960s theater that Sean and his theater company hope to revive. To bring attention to it, they created a Before I Die wall on the side of the theater, where it collected hopes to "meet my biological parents," "drive a race car," "find serenity," and "underestand who I am." "We believe that the lack of quality art in our city can also be considered a kind of neglect of our community," said Sean. "This is why we decided to build our own Before I Die wall." He didn't realize he would gain an additional role. "It seems I've become the Italian consultant for Before I Die. I have lots of people from all over Italy coming to me asking me how to do it."

made with love by MASSIMILIANO TAURINO, SEAN MICHAEL HALL, ALESSANDRO PERUFFO, PAOLO GUERRA, FORUM FERMENTO / CINEMA TEATRO PRIMAVERA - ASSOCIAZIONE CULTURALE ARCHIBUGIO A SALVE

238

Sophie Miller & Dan Blah Meredith

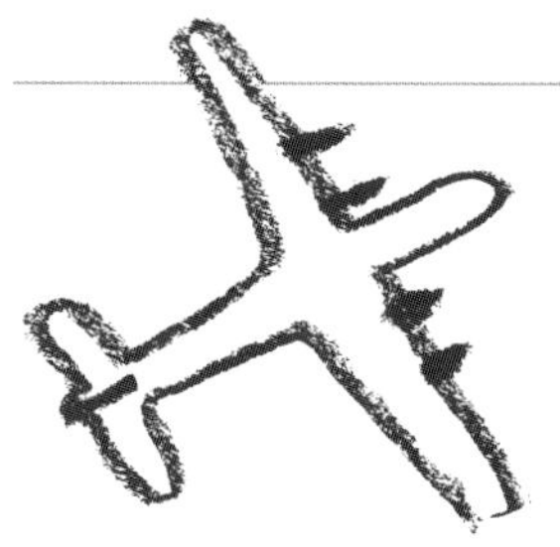

THE NATIONAL AIR AND SPACE MUSEUM IS THE MOST VISITED MUSEUM IN THE U.S.
BUILDINGS ARE NOT ALLOWED TO BE TALLER THAN 13 STORIES
POPULATION: 632,323

Washington D.C.

organized by
SOPHIE MILLER & DAN BLAH MEREDITH

This is a tender story about the ripple effects of generosity. When Travis' grandmother died, she left him some money and he created a small philanthropy circle with $1,000. He gave ten friends $100 each to spend as they liked. Sophie was one of those friends. She bought materials for a Before I Die wall and, with the help of Dan Blah Meredith, created it on the temporary construction barricade in front of a closed laundromat in Logan Circle. The wall stayed up for four months and soaked in hopes to "be on time," "become the U.S. Surgeon General," and "not be afraid to burn bridges." "One of my grandmothers had died a few months before, and we made the wall on the anniversary of my English grandmother's death." said Sophie. "I have no idea what they would have thought of the wall, but I see it as an homage to our three grandmothers, who were all pretty remarkable women."

made with love by SOPHIE MILLER AND DAN BLAH MEREDITH, WITH SPECIAL THANKS TO TRAVIS MOORE

Before I die I want to...

improvise with confidence.

Before I die I want to...

live in Detroit.

Before I die I want to...

take a commercial flight to the moon.

Before I die I want to...

remember my grandmother and her ideals.

Before I die I want to...

come to terms with who I am.

Belinda Kanpetch

Before I die I want to...

have
a storybook
ending.

Sophie Miller & Dan Blah Meredith

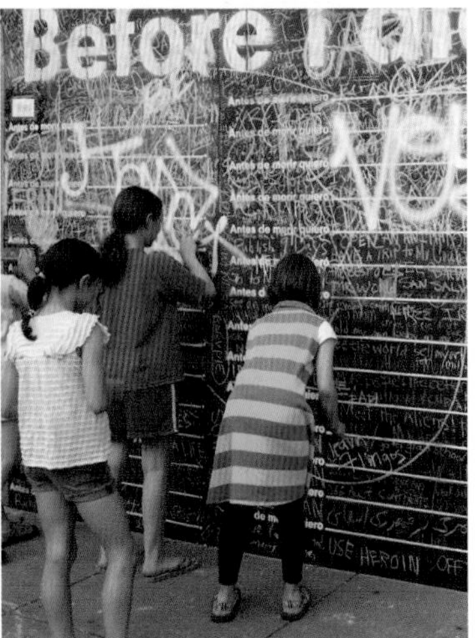

Before I die I want to...

see this building become a laundry again.

Belinda Kanpetch

Before I die I want to...

travel to 100 countries.

SORAYA'S STORY

Ever since studying abroad in college in 1999, I've been passionate about travel. I've gone on solo backpacking trips and trips with friends, family, and boyfriends. Each experience has been unique and memorable in its own way. So far, I've been to forty countries and have a goal of going to one hundred countries before I die. I want to see, hear, taste, and feel every corner of the world.

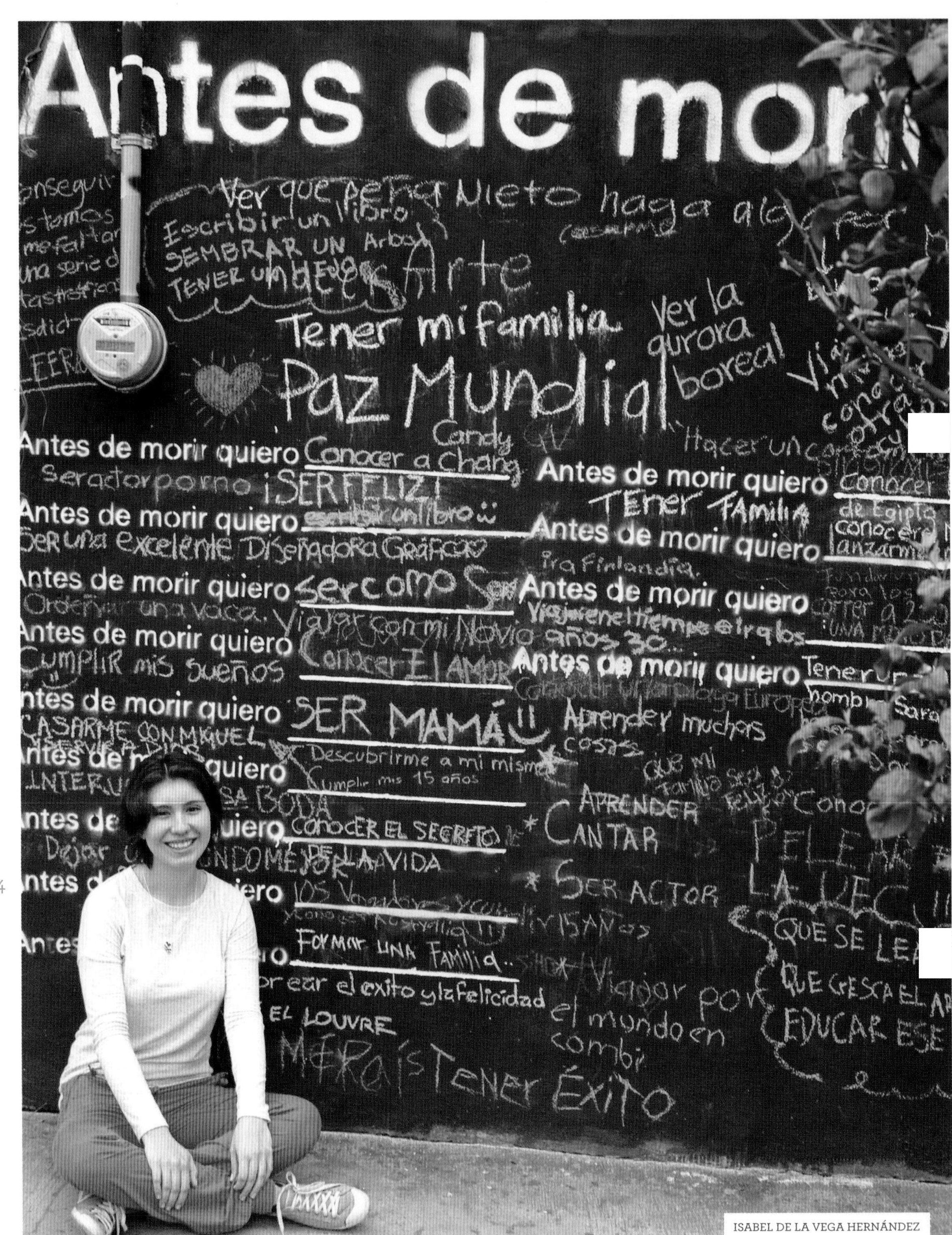

ISABEL DE LA VEGA HERNÁNDEZ

Adriana Hernández Álvarez

PRONOUNCED "JALAPA," JALAPENO PEPPERS WERE NAMED AFTER THE CITY
CALLED THE CITY OF FLOWERS
POPULATION: 413,136

Xalapa
Mexico

organized by
ISABEL DE LA VEGA HERNÁNDEZ

It only takes one determined girl to make a wall. When Isabel de la Vega Hernández learned about the Before I Die project, she coaxed her dad to buy painting materials. She cut her own stencil during breaks at school. And with her parents' permission, she installed it on the side of her family's house. Her mom helped and cheered her on throughout the process. Neighbors shared hopes to work in the Louvre, visit the Pyramids, and build a public school. As for Isabel, she could have easily filled the whole wall on her own. "The first thing I wrote on the wall was 'meet Candy Chang.' Then I wrote 'continue being happy,' 'watch the Northern Lights,' 'visit a European beach,' 'swim with a whale shark again,' 'make a quote that people remember, just like John Lennon did,' 'be an extra in a movie,' 'donate blood,' 'write on other Before I Die walls,' and 'milk a cow.' These are things that are meaningful to me and I know that as I grow older, I´ll add brand new things to my list."

made with love by JUANA ISABEL DE LA VEGA HERNÁNDEZ AND ADRIANA HERNÁNDEZ ÁLVAREZ

Remixes

Graeme Meyer

Washington D.C.

organized by
CITY YEAR

made with love by
JENNA LYKES, JENNIFER UPCHURCH, ISABEL HUSTON, ASHLEY MILLER, AND EVAN WALDT

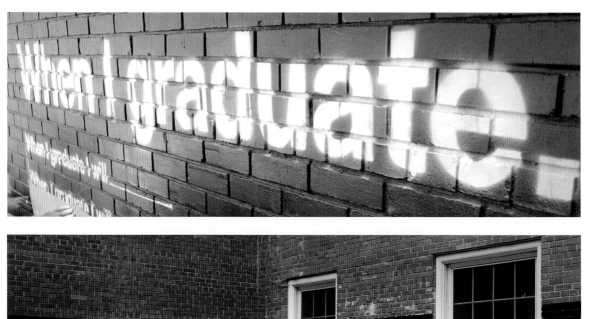

Sherif Maktabi

Beirut
LEBANON

organized by
PROJECT BETTER

made with love by
SHERIF MAKTABI AND KARIM BADRA

Candy Chang

250

San Francisco CALIFORNIA

organized by
LULULEMON SAN FRANCISCO

made with love by
LINDSAY JENSEN-EVANS, KALEIGH SHAFER, AND CIARA VIEHWEG

My dream is...

Gabriele Valente Feliz

Rio de Janeiro *BRAZIL*

organized by
CONHEÇA SEU VIZINHO

made with love by
GABRIELE VALENTE FELIZ, MARCELO ZISSU, CAIO CHACAL, ALINE CAMPBELL, AND NATA FAMÍLIA

Porto Alegre needs more...

PORTO ALEGRE PRECISA DE MAIS
EDUCAÇÃO!
carinho

PORTO ALEGRE PRECISA DE MAIS
RESPEITO
BOATE

Gabriel Medeiros Gomes

Porto Alegre *BRAZIL*

organized by
SHOOT THE SHIT

made with love by
GABRIEL GOMES, LUCIANO BRAGA, AND GIOVANI GROFF

Su Kahumbu

Nairobi *KENYA*

organized by

SU KAHUMBU & HER DAUGHTERS

made with love by

SU KAHUMBU, STEFANIE STEPHANOU, ELLENI STEPHANOU AND THE MONIKO'S RESTAURANT MANAGEMENT

Before I graduate I want to DRINK A LOT OF COFFEE.
Before I graduate I want to have a baby.
Before I graduate I want to have a 4some.

Before I graduate...
Before I graduate I want to
NHL

Wout Laban

Leeuwarden *NETHERLANDS*

organized by
CENTRAL PARK OFFICE

made with love by
WOUT LABAN AND TOM RAVESLOOT

We know they're inspired by it.

WOUT & TOM'S STORY

Right from the moment we saw the Before I Die project, we knew we had to do something with it. We decided to build our own wall at our school, Noordelijke Hogeschool Leeuwarden University, but change it a bit so it would fit better in the community. We changed the sentence to 'Before I graduate I want to...'

Within two hours all the spots on the wall were filled and people started to write outside the lines. At the end of every week we cleaned the wall, so everybody got a chance to write something. After a couple of weeks we realized we fully lost control of the wall and we started to accept it. The wall was living its own life and writing its own story.

After we took the wall down, we cut it up and gave the pieces away. It's an amazing feeling that people took a piece of the project home because we know they're inspired by it.

Savita Datt

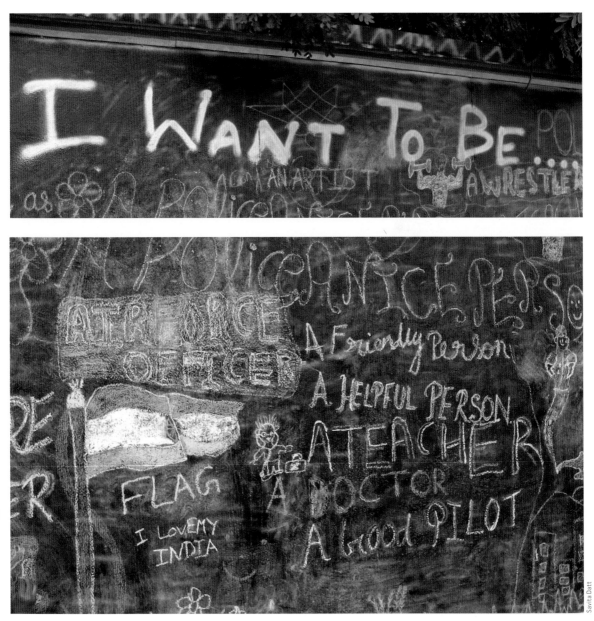

Faridabad
INDIA

organized by
PRAKASH DEEP SCHOOL

made with love by
SAVITA DATT, PRANJAL, KARAN, AND SANGEETA KHANDA

Holly Knoll

Tacoma WASHINGTON

organized by
SEONG SHIN

made with love by
SEONG SHIN, PAUL SPARKS, HOLLY KNOLL, TERESA PLACENTIA, IAN WHEELOCK, BEVERLY NAIDUS, RICK JONES, OWEN BOWER, PATRICIA LECY DAVIS, CLAIRE MENDENHAL, BRIAN LEHRER, TAMMY SCARLETT, AND BABE LEHLER

Lisa Kikuchi

Yamagata JAPAN

organized by
TOHOKU UNIVERSITY OF ART & DESIGN

made with love by
LISA KIKUCHI AND SHINO KOJIMA

Chad Buckwalter

Beijing *CHINA*

organized by

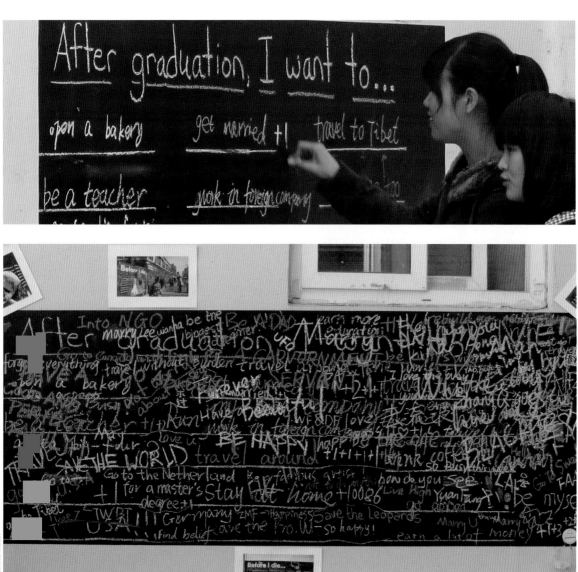

CHAD BUCKWALTER, THE BJ REVIEWER & BEIJING FORESTRY UNIVERSITY

made with love by

CHAD BUCKWALTER, JUN WANG, ESTHER WU, LUCY, JAMES, HANNAH, JIM, JENNIFER, HANNAH, TINA, ARTHUR, TONY, CARL, EASON, AND PETER

Jennifer Mcintyre

Vancouver *WASHINGTON*

organized by

FORT VANCOUVER HIGH SCHOOL

made with love by

SUMMER BAULEY, CHRISTIAN BRANNAN, DAVID BROWN, MAXWELL BURDICK, FREDY CAMPUZANO, DYLAN COONEY-LAND, HOPE CRIDER, DANNELL DEFRANCO, SONIA GASTELUM, VANESSA HANKE, SAMANTHA HOODENPYLE, JOSE HUERTA, JONATHON HUGHES, ASHLEI JONES, K-LAST KARUO, KAILA MCBRIDE, JULIO-CESAR MONTOYA, DIANA NARANJO, JAQUELINE PEREZ-SANDOVAL, CHRIS RANSON, WALTER ROBEDEAU, SHON ROTH, HAILIE ROWLAND, NOAH RUTLAND, DAMARIS SANCHEZ, SAUL SANCHEZ, KAMRA SHIELDS, JACOB ULREY, ANGELICA VALENCIA, MITCHELL WHITTEN, AND JENNIFER MCINTYRE

This idea sparked a passion.

JENNIFER'S STORY

I'm a first year teacher at a low income high school in Vancouver, Washington where students face an enormous amount of poverty and hardship. I've seen struggles that I never anticipated encountering in my life, and my heart has swelled for these kids. They need inspiration and motivation on a daily basis, and it's been a remarkable journey for me, as a young teacher, to discover ways of encouraging that.

One moment of inspiration came after my class watched Candy's TED talk about the Before I Die project. We began reflecting on the video, and the class completely exploded! They started talking about things they would like to do before they die, and pretty soon it morphed into complete and total chaos. It was a time in my short teaching career that I am very grateful that I let the class take over and allow myself to lose a bit of control, because what happened next was the greatest teaching moment I've had.

One of my students asked if we could grab a long sheet of paper from the library and make our own Before I Die poster to hang up and have kids around the school fill out between classes. It seemed like a great idea to me, so he went to get the paper. As soon as he came back, the class attacked the red sheet. They put a heading on it and started writing hopes and dreams I've never heard them express.

We hung up the project outside of our room at the end of class, and the kids have decided to take pictures every day after they leave my classroom to see what new dreams have been written. Now they're even talking about making this an independent community project. This idea sparked a passion in my students that I haven't seen in a long time.

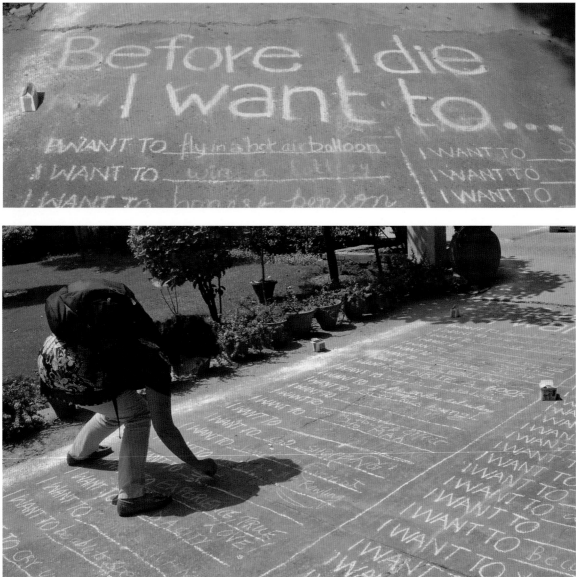

Sanaa Sohel Degani

Delhi
INDIA

organized by

YOUNG INDIA FELLOWSHIP PROGRAM

made with love by

SANAA DEGANI, MALINI BOSE, RINJU RAJAN, AARUSHI UBOWEJA, AARON BASAIAWMOIT, HARSH TRIPATHI, ADITYARAMAN S., AND ANUNAYA CHAUBEY

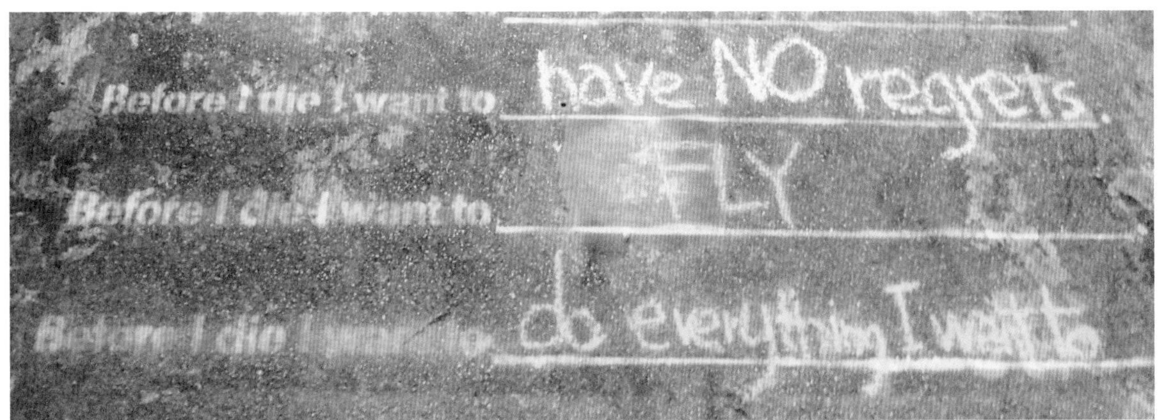

Dominique G. Nadeau

Hong Kong

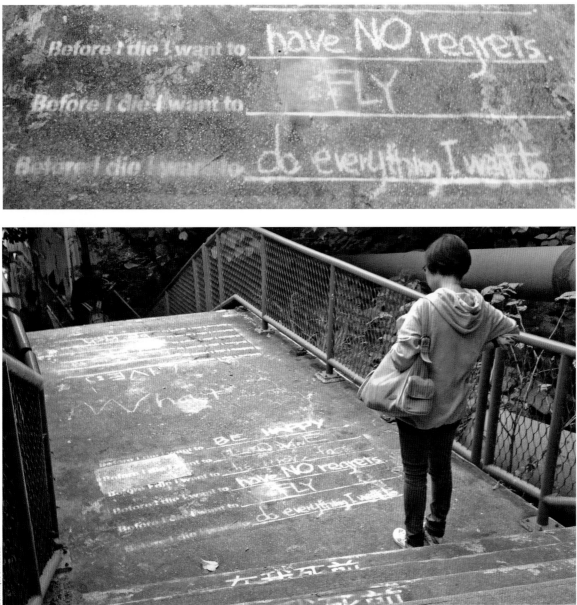

organized by
DOMINIQUE G. NADEAU

made with love by
DOMINIQUE G. NADEAU AND RONDA LEE

Anderson Petti

264

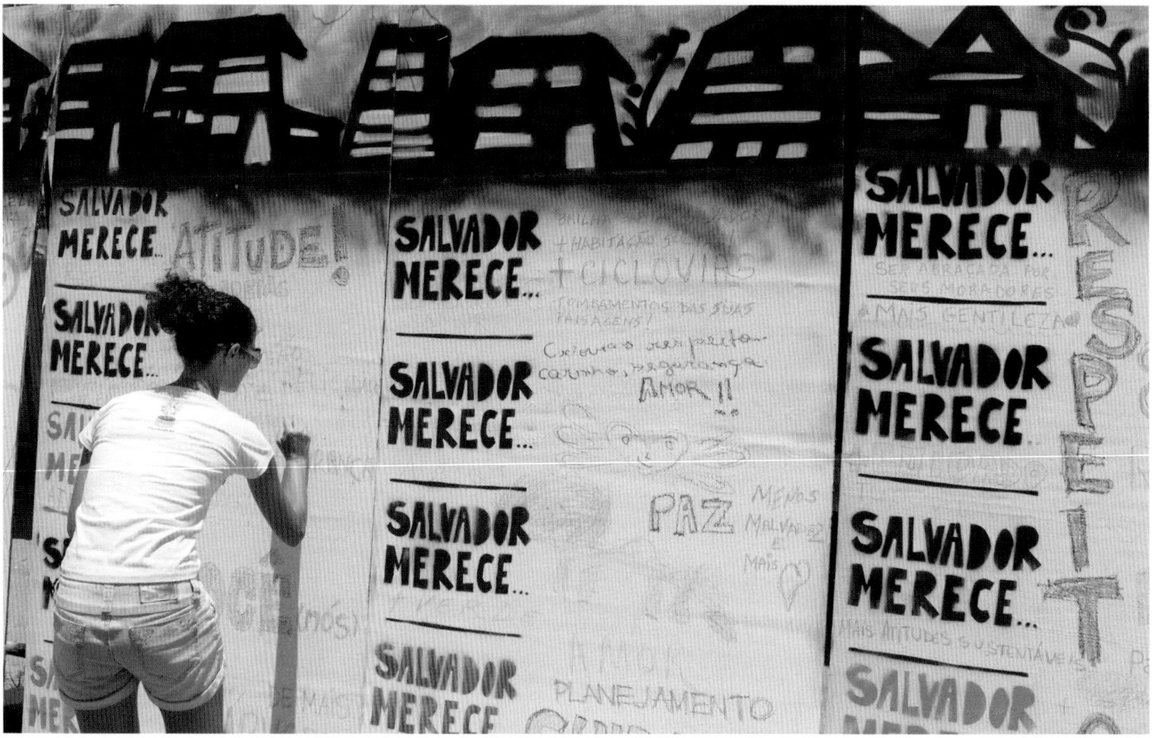

Salvador *BRAZIL*

organized by
CANTEIROS COLETIVOS AND BAIRRO-ESCOLA RIO VERMELHO

made with love by
THIAGO NAZARETH

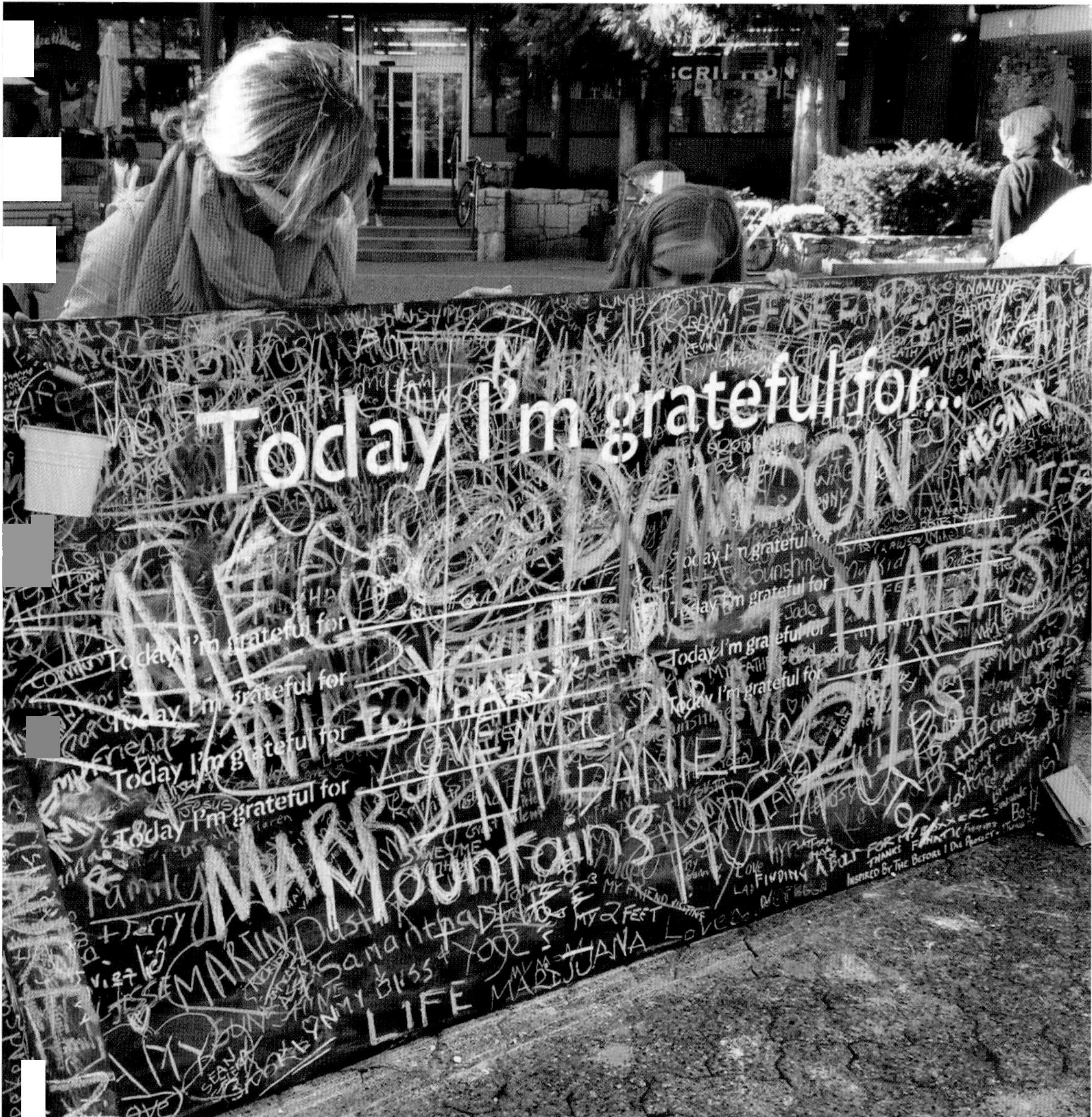

Dana Ramler

Vancouver CANADA

made with love by
DANA RAMLER

Don Spencer

USA

organized by
DON SPENCER

made with love by
DON SPENCER

I made people curious.

DON'S STORY

I've always been interested in cars, trucks, and motorcycles, which led me to volunteer at off-road races. I was on the course all the time where I prepped the vehicles. I was never a racer, but pretty close.

In 1999 my wife died of cancer. Later I was reacquainted with a childhood sweetheart and we got married. I still wanted to race and bought various types of vehicles to build, but it never happened. I didn't finish any of them.

All this time my second wife was in full support of my dreams. She was always encouraging me to just get one done. At the same time she was battling breast cancer. I supported her too at all her treatment and doctors' appointments. When her cancer grew worse, she fought on with a smile and an overwhelming need to make sure everyone else was okay. She assured us she would be fine until she was 99. She died June 9, 2011, and I was lost for sure.

Later that year, my church found out about the Before I Die project and put on a series of services called "Before I Die I want to." What a great idea, I thought. It motivated me to finish a project that was a long time coming. I was going to drive a race truck in an off-road race. I was going to ask others: "What do you want to do before you die?"

I painted my truck, trailer, and tow vehicle. Made some die cut vinyl. Made some stencils. Made my poster board. I went to three race venues that year. I made friends. I made people curious. I told my story and they told me theirs. I didn't win anything, but I finished putting a truck together and I raced.

By the Numbers

OVER 200 WALLS HAVE BEEN CREATED ON

6 CONTINENTS & 40+ COUNTRIES

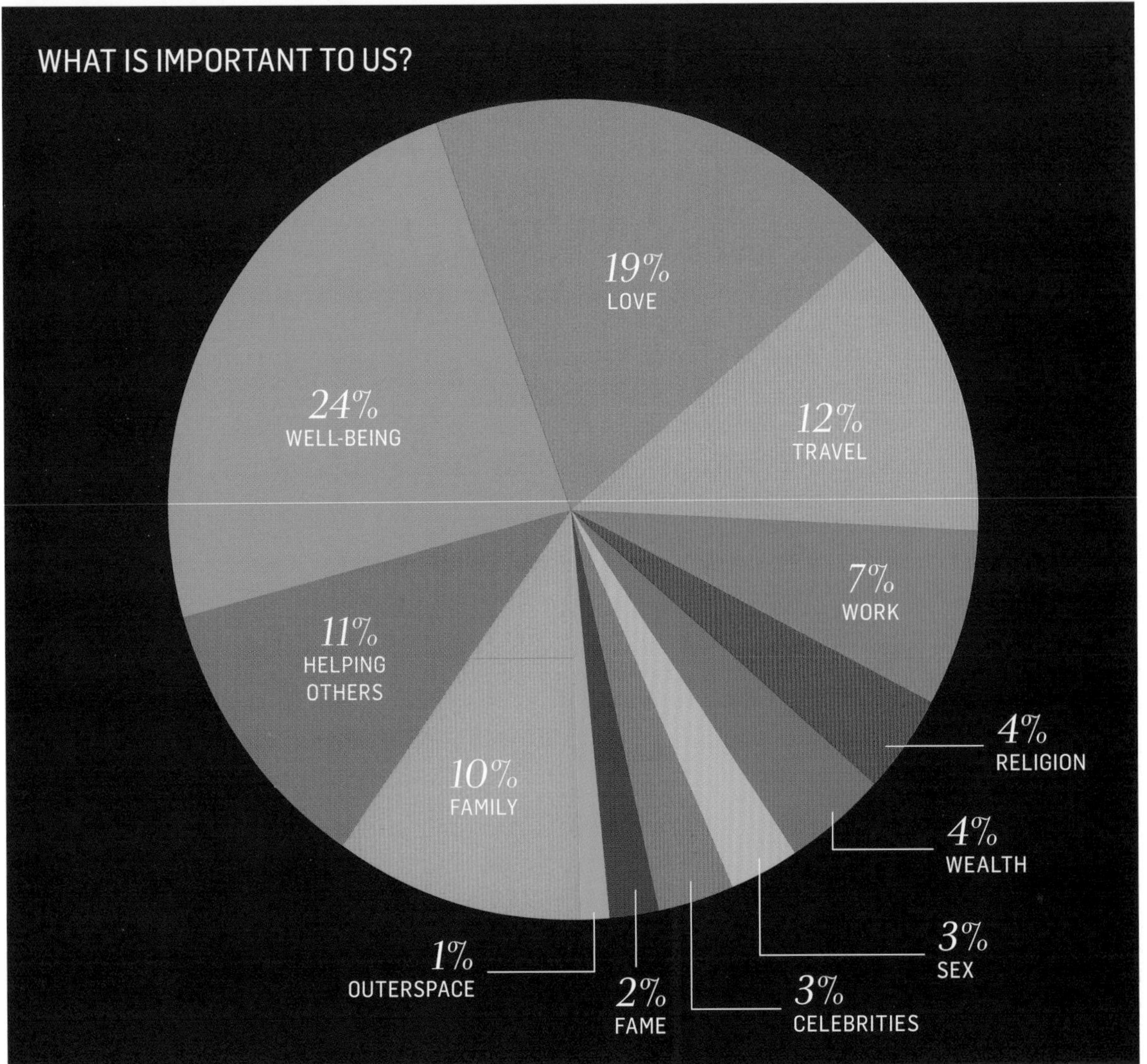

Based on over 100,000 responses from around the world

CITY SUPERLATIVES

Most romantic	SAVANNAH
Most sex on the brain	THE NETHERLANDS
Cares most about family	QUERÉTARO
Most excited to travel the world	MELBOURNE
Most worried about money	BROOKLYN
Most concerned with self improvement	MONTREAL
Most religious	MINNEAPOLIS
Biggest fan of celebrities	ALMATY
Just wants to be happy	LISBON

WALLS HAVE BEEN STENCILED IN 16+ LANGUAGES:

Afrikaans
VOORDAT EK STERF...

Arabic
قبل أن أموت

Chinese
...在我死之前

Danish
FØR JEG DØR

English
BEFORE I DIE...

Filipino
BAGO MAMATAY AKO

French
AVANT DE MOURIR...

German
BEVOR ICH STERBE MÖCHTE ICH...

Guaraní
AMANO MBOYVE...

Italian
PRIMA DI MORIRE...

Kazakh
МЕН ЕМЛРДЕН КЕТКЕНШЕ

Korean
내가 죽기 전에

Portuguese
ANTES DE MORRER...

Russian
ПРЕЖДЕ ЧЕМ Я УМРУ...

Spanish
ANTES DE MORIR...

Zulu
PHAMBI KOKUTHINGIFE...

TOP FIVE MOST COMMON RESPONSES GLOBALLY

1. *Love*
2. *Live*
3. *Travel*
4. *Be Happy*
5. *Help Others*

MOST UNUSUAL RESPONSES

Before I die I want to...

cycle across Africa

see our sparkly souls collide

swim in a pool of golden retriever puppies

heal people through neuroscience

see what I'm like as an old man

drive a cab for a day

get dressed and leave the house without looking in a single mirror

do nude backflips on the moon

win the solar decathlon

name a mountain

write a book, plant a tree, have a child

eat gelato every day for a year

be a wolf among the sheep
see America have a decent cable news station
write my own theory
kill the bastard that steals my sleeping bags
not be afraid to burn bridges
start our own porn company for females
canoe Lewis and Clark's route
live in neon
have a moonlight picnic
be a stripper and a nun at the same time
find a pearl in an oyster
travel the world by foot

EVEN MORE WALLS

Aarhus, Denmark

Brighton, United Kingdom

Budapest, Hungary

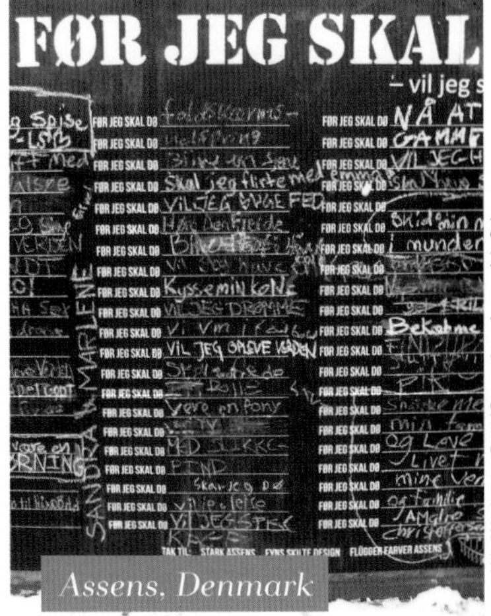

Assens, Denmark

Boston, Massachusetts

Amsterdam, Netherlands

Clockwise from top left: Michael Kristen Kristensen, Zak Finn, Martin Pedersen, Mikel Verhagen, David Bresnahan, Annamária Schnetz

Buffalo, New York

Cebu City, Philippines

Campinas, Brazil

Cordoba, Spain

Bishop, California

Crete, Nebraska

Clockwise from top left: Patrick Finan/Block Club, Radel Paredes, Angel Thomas, Kristina Kassem, Jerry Oser, Julio Malosso Jr. Fotografia

Denver, Colorado

Dubai, United Arab Emirates

Daegu, South Korea

278

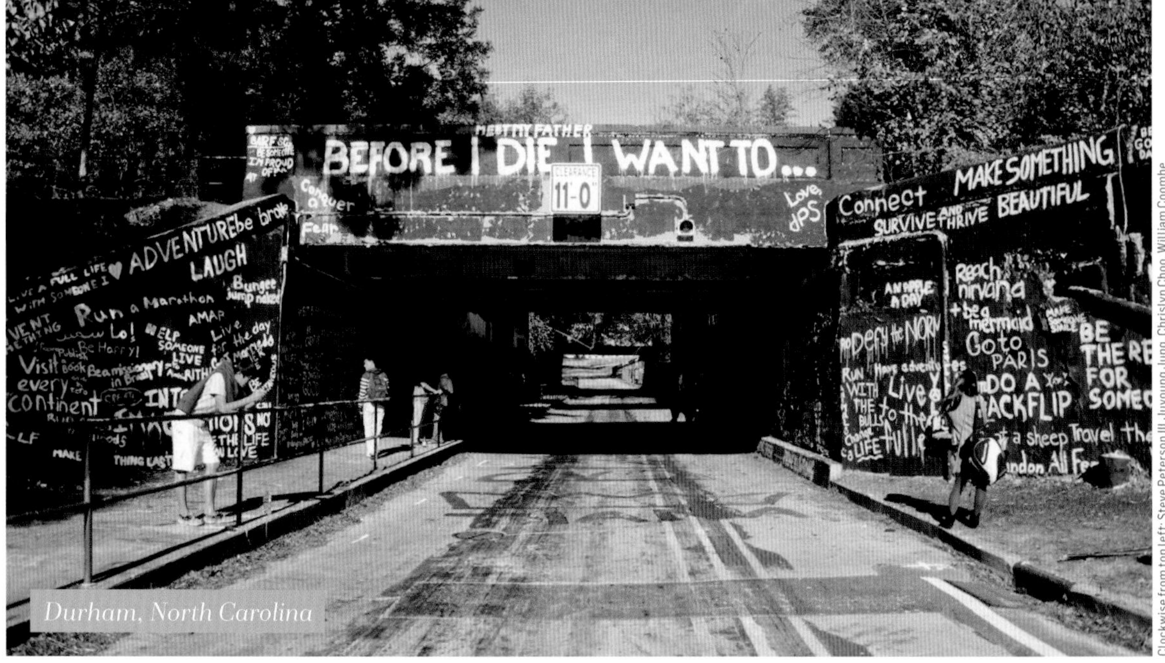

Durham, North Carolina

Clockwise from top left: Steve Peterson III, Juyoung Jung, Chrislyn Choo, William Coombe

Hefei, China

Herzliya, Israel

Geraldton, Australia

Glasgow, Scotland

High Wycombe, United Kingdom

Guatemala City, Guatemala

Clockwise from top left: Yao Yuhang, TEDxIDC, Jonny Harris/Playdead Ltd., Alejandro Morales, Paula Brotto, Sarah Andrews

Hoboken, New Jersey

Innsifill, Canada

Jiangsu Province, China

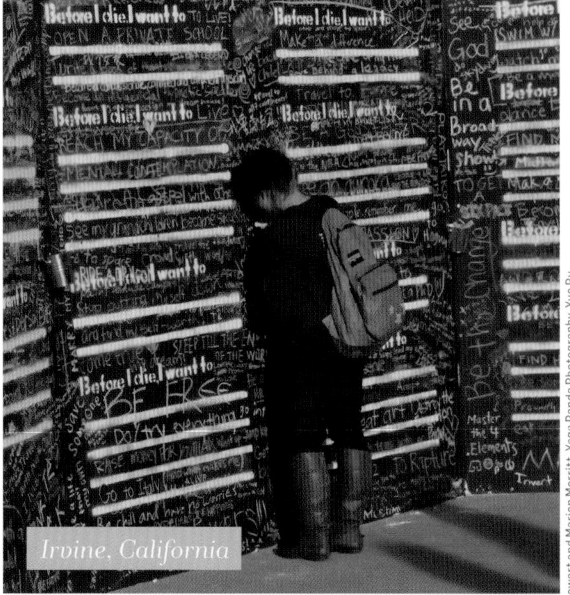

Irvine, California

Mount Vernon, Washington

Kansas City, Missouri

Clockwise from top left: Erin Hopson, Susan Downs, Kendrick Wang, Ann Stewart and Marion Merritt, Yoga Panda Photography, Yue Ru

Lantzville, BC, Canada

Kézdivásárhely, Romania

LaGrange, Georgia

London, United Kingdom

London, Ontario, Canada

Long Beach, California

Clockwise from top left: Kavita Maharaj, Zoltán Cserei, Dean Rogers, Cat Halloaker, Candy Chang, Lauren Currie

Acapulco, Mexico

Millis, Massachusetts

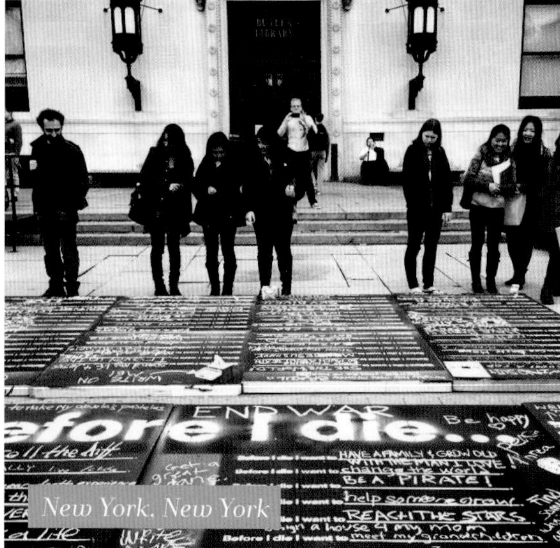

New York, New York

New Haven, Connecticut

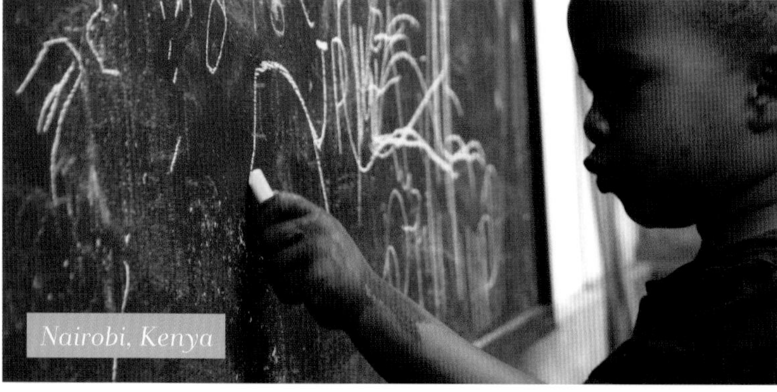

Nairobi, Kenya

Riyadh, Saudi Arabia

Clockwise from top left: Guadalupe Hernández, Ian Matthews, Uma Ramiah, Fadwa Almutlaq, Anthony Wachira Mwangi, No Credit

Oro Valley, Arizona

Raleigh, North Carolina

Philadelphia, Pennsylvania

Salem, Oregon

San Antonio, Texas

Clockwise from top left: Michael Wifall, Teresa Pigeon, Sean Whener, Raleigh Rapier, Brian Hart

San Diego, California

Santa Cruz, California

Sulmona, Italy

Singapore

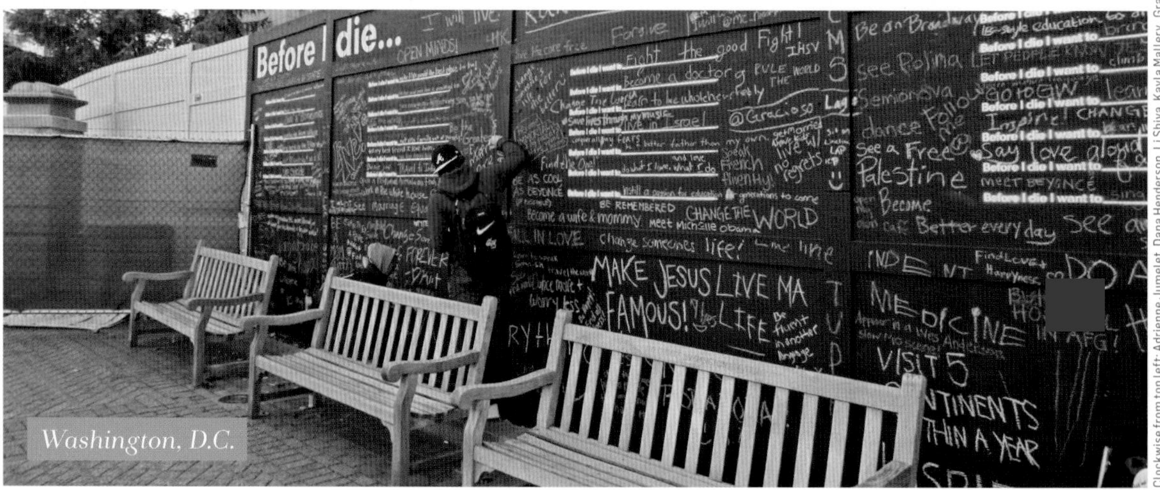

Washington, D.C.

Clockwise from top left: Adrienne Jumelet, Dana Henderson, Li Shiya, Kayla Mallery, Graziano Tullio

Wilmington, Delaware

Wolverhampton, United Kingdom

Zurich, Switzerland

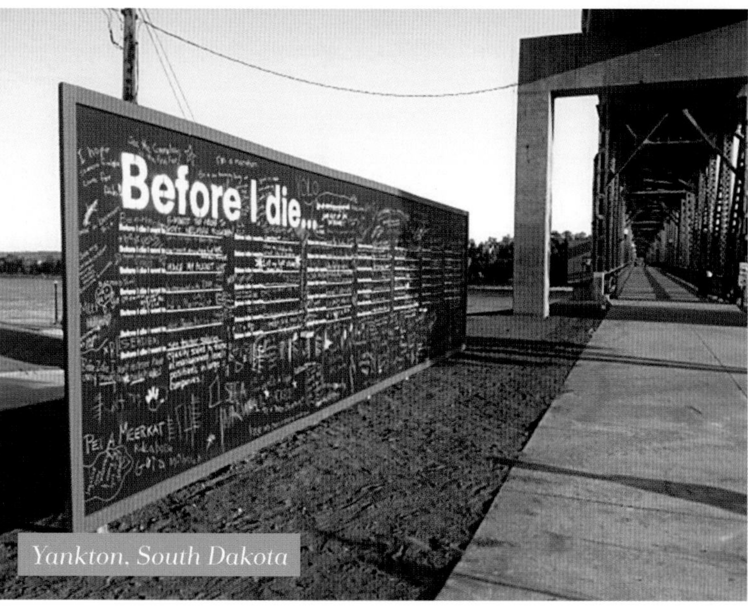

Yankton, South Dakota

Winter Garden, Florida

Clockwise from top left: Marlene Rusnak, Debbie Shelley, Dana Allar & Lihi Ben Haim & Olga Bushkova, Izumi Sakurada, Sarah Mannes Homstad

How to make a wall

Anyone can build a Before I Die wall! It's fun and a great way to get involved in your community. You simply need a wall, some chalkboard paint, a few boxes of chalk, white spray-paint, and a stencil. Preparing the stencil is the trickiest part. I created the stencil for the first Before I Die wall by printing out the text, pasting it to a piece of poster board, and cutting each letter with a blade. This took some time, but it's certainly doable. Since then, I've had stencils made by a stencil manufacturer. A one-column stencil makes it much faster to stencil, and a thick mylar material makes it easy to hang your stencil rigid to a wall with minimal tape.

In addition to preparing the materials to build your wall, it's just as important to find a suitable location, obtain permission, and invite the community to participate. Continue reading to learn more about building a wall of your own.

Example walls

TO STIR YOUR MIND

Below are examples of Before I Die walls in other cities to show you different ways people have created their own walls. There's no right or wrong way; just the way that works for you and your community.

Temporary construction barrier
Brooklyn, New York

Side of building
Lisbon, Portugal

Plywood attached to fence
Reno, Nevada

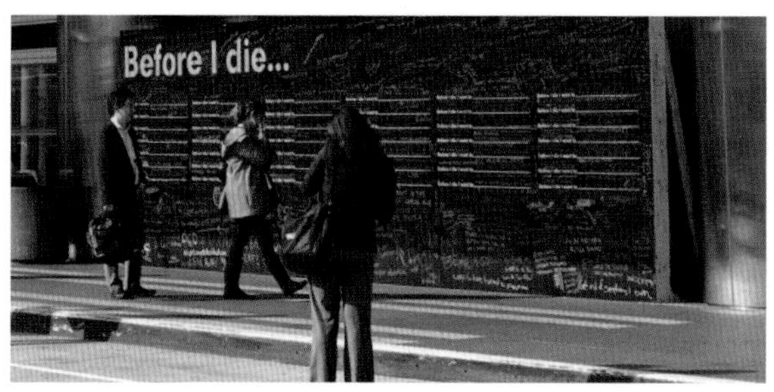

Freestanding plywood wall
San Francisco, California

Plywood leaning against building
Montreal, Canada

Standalone structure
Townsville, Australia

What you'll need

A HANDY CHECKLIST

- ☐ COLUMN STENCIL

Before I die...

- ☐ TITLE STENCIL

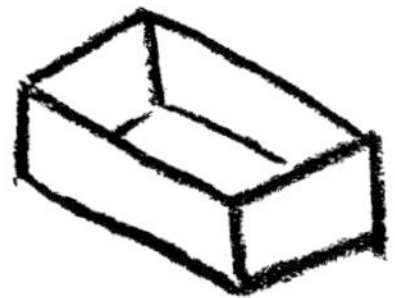

- ☐ CHALK HOLDERS

- ☐ CHALKBOARD PAINT

- ☐ WHITE SPRAY PAINT

- ☐ PAINT TRAYS

- ☐ MEASURING TAPE

- ☐ DUCT TAPE

- ☐ SPONGE MOP

Below is a handy checklist of materials to make your Before I Die wall. The costs will vary depending on the size of your wall and the cost of local materials. A 24 x 8 foot (7.3 x 2.4 meter) wall requires 6-8 cans of chalkboard paint and 4 cans of spray paint. The amount of chalk you'll need will depend on how long your wall is up. You don't need a big budget to make a big impact!

- ☐ CHALK

- ☐ GLOVES

- ☐ TARP

- ☐ PAINT ROLLERS

- ☐ PAINT BRUSHES

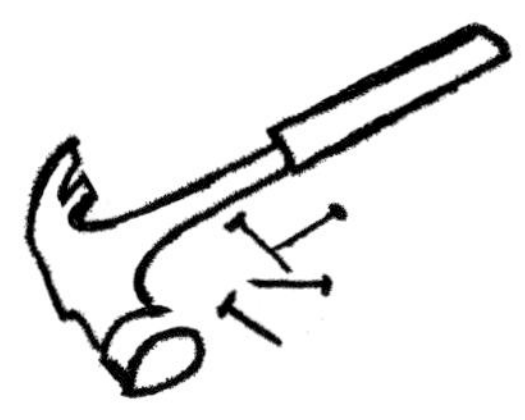

- ☐ HAMMER & NAILS

- ☐ BUCKET

- ☐ WIFI

- ☐ CAMERA

To Do List

FOR BUILDING YOUR BEFORE I DIE WALL

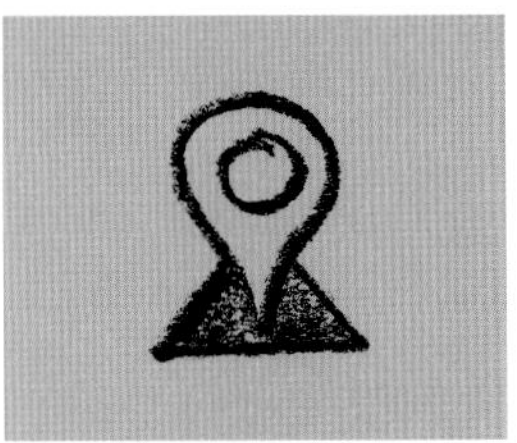

CHOOSE A SITE

A good location has regular foot traffic. Once you find an ideal location, find out who owns the property and see what they think of the idea. People have painted on construction barriers, sides of buildings, and interior walls. They've also built plywood walls and attached them to fences or placed them in plazas, campuses, and parks. A wall can be created by one person, but it's easier if you have help! People have created walls with friends, family, neighbors, classmates, coworkers, and organizations who can help provide a space or other resources.

GET PERMISSION

Public spaces are for everyone, and it's important to respect the community where you plan to install your wall. A good way to obtain permission is by speaking with people who live and work near the site you've chosen, such as the owner of the property, local community groups, and business owners and residents in the area. Every city has different rules concerning public art, so consider partnering with a local organization who can help you with this process.

SPREAD THE WORD

Select a date for your "ribbon-cutting" and spread the word. Most importantly, inform the people who live and work around the wall so they know what's happening. People have used social media, print and online publications, local organizations, mailing lists, and flyers to organize and promote their wall.

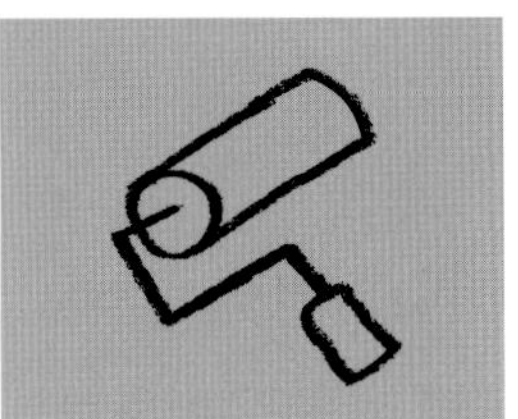

MAKE YOUR WALL

We've included a checklist of materials and general costs, which will depend on your wall size and structure. A typical wall can take a day or two to paint and stencil. Depending on the weather, the chalkboard paint can take several hours to thoroughly dry. In the following pages you'll find a step-by-step guide to help you on installation day.

MAINTAIN & SHARE

Check on your wall frequently to take care of it and document responses. A few thoughtful responses will set the tone for your wall. If there is anything inappropriate, just erase it. Once the wall is full, wash it with water to start fresh again. Take lots of photos and share them!

Wall Layout

HELPFUL NOTES FOR PLANNING YOUR LAYOUT

Depending on the size of your wall, the number of columns and spacing will vary. Our wall in New Orleans was 41 feet (12.5 meters) long and comfortably fit 10 columns. Keep in mind space to fit chalk holders. We suggest two on either end and maybe more in between if your wall is long. The diagram below is an example of how a 24 foot long wall could look like. Feel free to do what feels right for you.

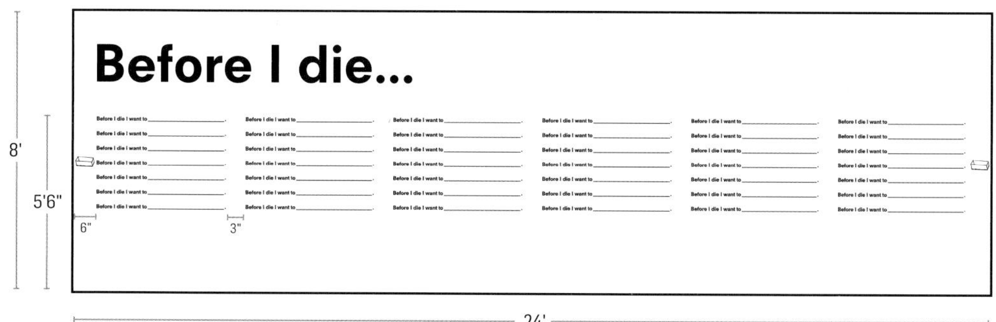

Stencil Dimensions

THE HEIGHT & WIDTH OF YOUR STENCILS

293

Here are the dimensions of the stencils we've used to help you figure out how to lay out your wall. The font is Neuzeit Book Heavy with -25 kerning.

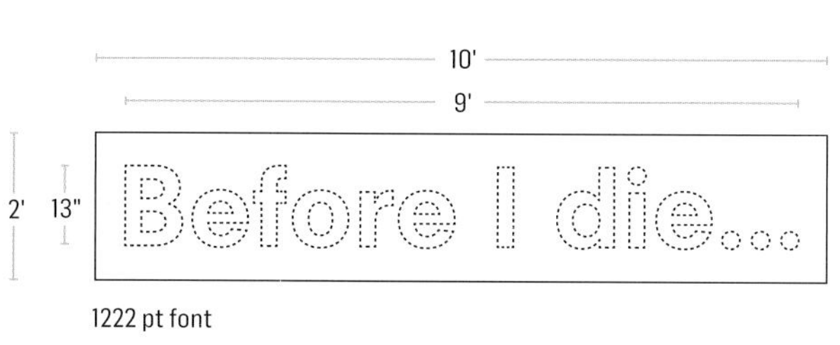

1222 pt font

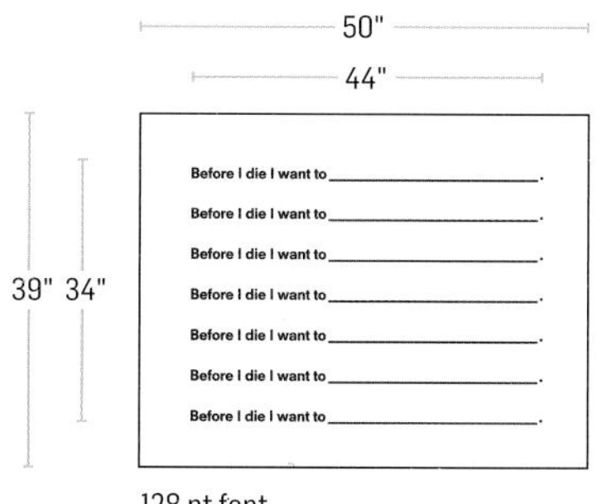

128 pt font

Kristina Kassem

what you'll need

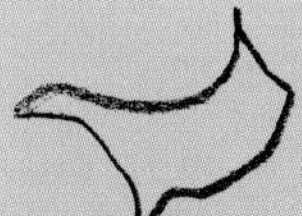
TARP

CHALKBOARD PAINT

PAINT TRAY

PAINT ROLLER

PAINT BRUSH

Prepare & paint

Lay tarp (or any cheap material with a large surface area) on the ground in front of your wall to keep it free of paint. Using a paint roller, apply two coats of chalkboard paint. Use a paint brush or sponge brush to fill in any unpainted cracks. Take a break and let the paint dry.

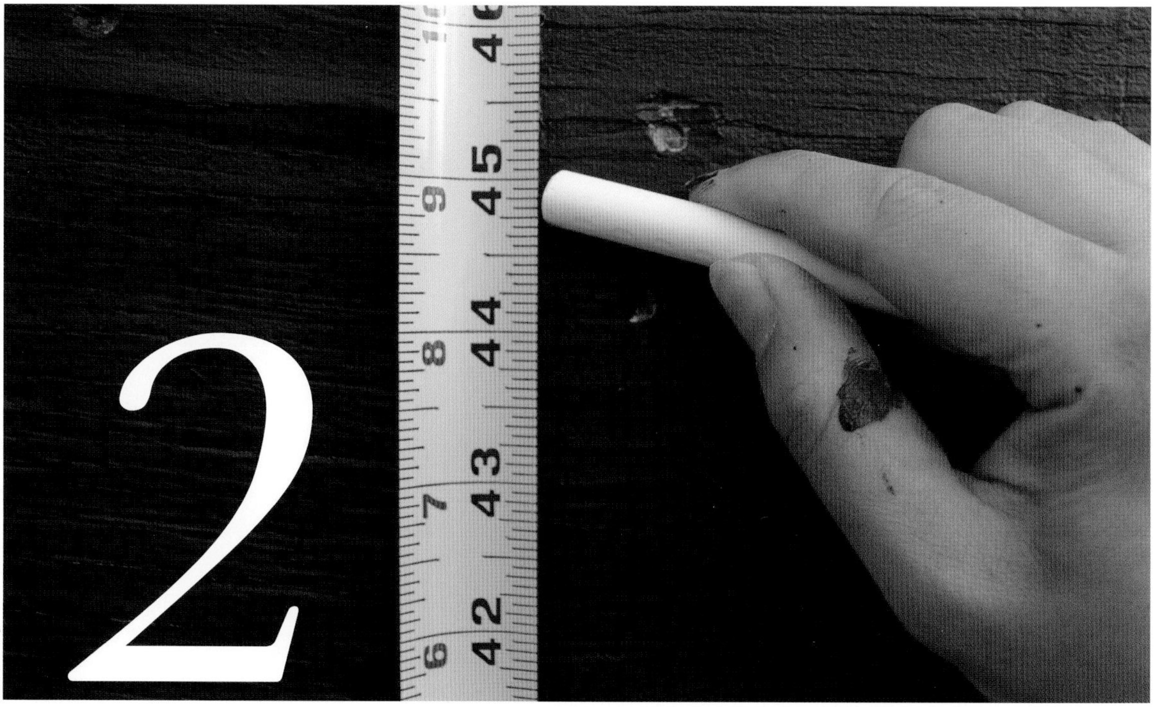

Candy Chang

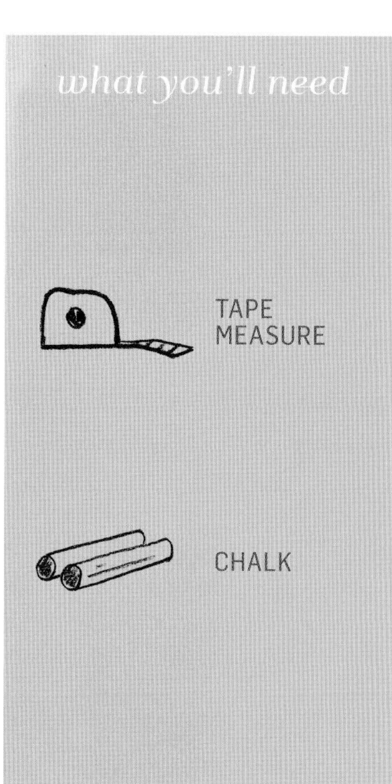

2 Measure & mark

Measure and mark the placement of your stencils so they will be evenly distributed across your wall and at a comfortable height. A piece of string or chalk line can help you create a horizontal line to align your stencil. Remember space for chalk holders.

3

Candy Chang

what you'll need
TARP
COLUMN STENCIL
Before I die...
TITLE STENCIL
DUCT TAPE
GLOVES
SPRAY PAINT

Stencil

Line up your stencil to your markings and tape it to the wall. Shake your spray paint can for at least one minute before using, and then spray in light strokes. A little goes a long way and too much might make it drippy. Shake your spray paint can throughout the process. Hold the stencil down with your other hand to help make crisp lines. You can always use chalkboard paint to touch it up later.

Mark Hammon

4

what you'll need

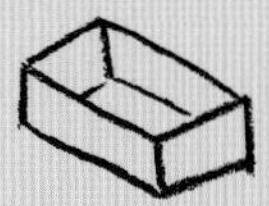

CHALK HOLDERS

HAMMER AND NAILS

CHALK

Add chalk

Attach chalk holders with nails or screws and make sure they are securely fastened to the wall. You can use any weather-proof container that allows rain to pass through. Add colorful sticks of chalk and let the sharing begin! Leave a thoughtful response or two to set the tone and stir the minds of passersby.

5

Camdy Chang

what you'll need

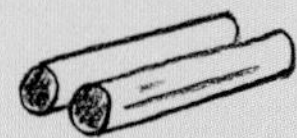

CHALK

SPONGE MOP

BUCKET

Maintain

Check on your wall frequently to document responses, provide more chalk, and keep it clean. If there is anything inappropriate, just erase it. When the wall is completely filled, wash it off using a wet sponge mop or towel so more people can share their hopes and dreams too.

Candy Chang

6

what you'll need

CAMERA

INTERNET ACCESS

Document & share

Take lots of photos of your wall and share them with others! We've provided a step-by-step guide to help you document and share your wall online. Learn more at beforeidie.cc.

COPY THIS SPREAD AT 1000% TO GET A FULL SIZE TEMPLATE FOR CREATING YOUR WALL, OR USE THIS PAGE TO RECORD YOUR OWN DREAMS.

Before I die I want to ______________________________.

Before I die I want to ______________________________.

Before I die I want to ______________________________.

Before I die I want to ______________________________.

Before I die I want to ______________________________.

Before I die I want to ______________________________.

Before I die I want to ______________________________.

Before I die I want to ______________________________.

Before I die I want to ______________________________.

Before I die I want to ______________________________.

Before I die I want to ______________________________.

Before I die I want to ______________________________.

Before I die I want to ______________________________.

Before I die I want to ______________________________.

Before I die I want to ______________________________.

Before I die I want to ______________________________.

Before I die I want to ______________________________.

Before I die I want to ______________________________.

Before I die I want to ______________________________.

Before I die I want to ______________________________.

Before I die I want to ______________________________.

Before I die I want to ______________________________.

Before I die I want to ______________________________.

Before I die I want to ______________________________.

Before I die

Before I die I want to ________________.

Before I die I want to ________________.

Before I die I want to ________________.

Before I die I want to ________________.

Before I die I want to ________________.

Before I die I want to ________________.

Before I die I want to ________________.

Before I die I want to ________________

Before I die I want to ________________

Before I die I want to ________________

Before I die I want to ________________

Before I die I want to ________________

Before I die I want to ________________

Before I die I want to ________________

LOVE. LIKE. CHRIST.
Dearest to Me
Make a name
Make a difference!
I want to live
Be a friend
Before I die I want to
Before I die I want to
Before I die I want to
TITANIC
Before I die I want to
See a glacier!
become a sister wife
LIVE
I WANT TO
Before I die I want to
GO SKYDIVING
buy new underwear
Before I die I want to
Feel complete
Before I die I want to
PHOTOGRAPH A MOVEMENT
FALL IN LOVE
Before I die I want to
Go to Japan
I want to
LIVE
CHANGE A LIFE
#BIDSAV
I want to accomplish
TRULY
LIVE!
MY PURP
I want to MEET
my father
I want to leave
my mark on
the world.♡ -Cecily
LIVE!
See World Peace
Before I die I want everyone to be happy
Live
I've Dr
ed Of
WILL NEVER
Camdy Chang

Before I die I want to ______________________________.

Before I die I want to ______________________________.

Before I die I want to ______________________________.

Before I die I want to ______________________________.

Before I die I want to ______________________________.

Before I die I want to ______________________________.

Before I die I want to ______________________________.

Before I die I want to ______________________________.

Before I die I want to ______________________________.

Before I die I want to ______________________________.